THE AFRICAN CONDITION

To my sons
Let there be light!
Amen

The African Condition
A POLITICAL DIAGNOSIS

ALI A. MAZRUI

Director, Center for Afroamerican and African Studies
and Professor of Political Science,
University of Michigan, Ann Arbor

CAMBRIDGE UNIVERSITY PRESS
London
Cambridge   New York   New Rochelle
Melbourne   Sydney

Published in the USA and Canada by the Press Syndicate of the
University of Cambridge
32 East 57th Street, New York, N Y 10022, USA

First published 1980
Reprinted 1980,

Printed in the United States of America
Typeset by the Castlefield Press, High Wycombe, England
Printed and bound by Hamilton Printing Company, Rensselaer, New York

Library of Congress Catalog Number: 79-9657

ISBN 0 521 23265 1 hard covers
ISBN 0 521 29884 9 paperback

CONTENTS

This lecture examines the paradox that Africa is the first habitat of man but is the last to be made truly habitable. The crisis of habitability in recent history ranges from problems of tropical diseases to difficulties in physical communications and transportation, and from political instability in black Africa to the complexities of white-dominated southern Africa. The resulting exodus of refugees from both black tyranny and white racism is part of the crisis of 'living conditions' in a political sense. If Africa was Adam's birthplace, the Garden of Eden today is in serious disrepair. What is wrong?

Africans are not the most brutalized of peoples but are probably the most humiliated in modern history. In terms of physical brutalization, the holocaust suffered by the Jews under the Nazis and the genocidal treatment which native Americans and native Australians received from white people, were as gruesome as anything experienced by black people. But Africans have been humiliated in history in ways that range from the slave trade to being segregated and treated as third-class citizens in parts of their own continent to the present day, in spite of being numerically the majority. But racism as a social phenomenon is on the way out. Tribalism died first in Europe and will one day die in Africa. Racism is dying first in Africa and will one day come to an end in Europe as well. Human society will never be classless, but it will be detribalized and cured of racism.

LECTURE 3   A Clash of Cultures   46

African societies are not the closest to the West culturally but have been experiencing the most rapid pace of westernization this century. The continent is controlled disproportionately by westernized Africans. Christianity has spread faster in Africa than in any other continent. Acceptance of European languages for national business is greater in Africa than Asia. African educational institutions continue to be mechanisms for further westernization. Africans are caught up between rebellion against the West and imitation of the West. The continent has become a melting pot of different moral, cultural and intellectual systems. Does Africa need to be re-Africanized?

LECTURE 4 The Burden of Underdevelopment   70

Africa is not the poorest of the regions of the world in resources but it is the least developed of the inhabited continents. Immense mineral wealth and agricultural potential coexist with some of the lowest standards of living in the world. Part of the problem lies in the nature of the economic change which Western colonialism fostered in Africa. African economies were distorted to serve western needs. The coming economic struggle in Africa includes a search for ways to correct this distortion and overcome dependence. Seven strategies for transcending dependence need to be tried out, ranging from local self-reliance to the use of an economic Trojan horse to infiltrate the northern citadels of industrial might.

LECTURE 5   Patterns of Identity   90

Africa is not the smallest of the continents but it is probably the most fragmented. It is fragmented along ethnic, linguistic, religious, ideological and class lines. In addition a continent of less than 500 million people is split up into more than fifty nations, many of them tiny. This fragmentation is a handicap in Africa's struggle for social and material improvement. It also creates a security risk. Africa has to choose between, on the one hand, a system of international vigilantism, like Tanzania's punitive invasion of Uganda, and, on the other, a new continental system of collective security, possibly under the Organization of African Unity.

LECTURE 6 In Search of *Pax Africana*   113

Africa is the most central of all continents in geographical location, but politically and to some extent militarily it may be the most marginal. Physically it is cut almost in half by the Equator. It is also the only continent traversed by the Tropics of both Cancer and Capricorn. Economically

INTRODUCTION

A few years ago a sardonic reviewer of one of my books warned me that, if I did not look out, I would be invited to give the BBC Reith Lectures. I suppose the reviewer was in part referring to the style of my writing, caught between the formal and the informal, the rigorous and the casual, careful scholarship and polemical argument. Such an intermediate style is what Reith Lecturers are made of, ranging from Bertrand Russell to John Kenneth Galbraith.

I suppose one reason for this eclecticism is that the actual lectures are themselves caught up in the dilemma between reaching a mass audience and communicating with a more specialized intelligentsia. The academic prestige of the lectures pulls the writer towards jargon and specialized vocabulary. On the other hand, the fact that millions of people, in different parts of the world, are likely to hear the broadcasts demands sensitivity to a broad mass audience. It is a major challenge. I congratulate for sheer prescience my sardonic reviewer of several years ago who warned me about the Ides of Reith.[1]

My links with the British Broadcasting Corporation are much older than these lectures. The links go back to my student days at Nuffield College, Oxford. My girl-friend lived in London. Unknowingly, the BBC kept the "betrothal" warm by paying for my transportation to London once or twice every week. The Corporation invited me to give a virtually regular news commentary in both English and Swahili on the BBC African

[1] See R. W. Johnson's review of my book *Soldiers and Kinsmen in Uganda*, in *Political Studies* (Journal of the Political Studies Association of the United Kingdom) (1976), Vol. XXV No. 3, September 1977.

Service. The commuting between Oxford and London on BBC business constitutes part of the background to my subsequent marriage to Molly.

With regard to the domestic services of the BBC (no "domestic" pun intended), my involvement also goes back to my student days at Oxford. The Third Programme of the BBC invited me in 1963 to give two talks on Africa, one on what I called "The African Innocence" and the other on "The Dress of African Thought".

My links with the Corporation have never been completely broken since then, but the thought of being invited to be Reith Lecturer never occurred to me until that mischievous reviewer in *Political Studies* put the idea into my head.

The BBC's tentative exploration came when I was Visiting Professor of Modern Commonwealth History at the University of Leeds. I was asked by an official of the BBC if I would let my name go forward as one of the candidates for the 1979 Reith Lectures. The outcome of that exploration are these lectures.

These lectures are about location in space and allocation in society. They are concerned with Africa's physical position on the globe in relation to issues of economic distribution and social justice.

There is a sense in which Africa is both the centre of the world and the middle sector of the Third World. Yet the continent is only just entering the main stream of international history. Why this anomaly? Why has this central continent been so politically peripheral for so long?

Let us first explore in what sense Africa has been at the centre of the world. And how have these contiguities of Africa's geography influenced the contiguities of its history? In what ways has Africa's physical location conditioned its cultural and political destiny? Let us look more closely at these frontiers of political geography and cultural history as part of the broad background to these lectures.

Of the three ancient continents of Asia, Africa and Europe, Africa has again often played the role of a link, and sometimes mediator, between the Occident and the Orient. In history it has never been quite clear whether Africa was indeed part of the Orient or whether it should be included in the universe of the Occidentals.

So ambivalent has the status of this continent been that its northern portion, North Africa, has changed identity a number of times across the centuries. At one time North Africa was an extension of Europe. This goes back to the days of Carthage, of Hellenistic colonization, and later of the Roman Empire. The concept of Europe was at best in the making at that time. In the words of historians R. R. Palmer and Joel Colton: "There was really no Europe in ancient times. In the Roman Empire we may see a Mediterranean world, or even a West and an East in the Latin-and-Greek-speaking portions. But the West included parts of Africa as well as of Europe . . ."[2]

Even as late as the seventeenth century the idea that the land mass south of the Mediterranean was something distinct from the land mass north of it was a proposition still difficult to comprehend. The great American Africanist, Melville Herskovits, has pointed out how the Geographer Royal of France, writing in 1656, described Africa as "a peninsula so large that it comprises the third part, and this the most southerly, of our continent".[3]

This old proposition that North Africa was the southern part of Europe had its last desperate fling in the modern world in France's attempt to keep Algeria as part of France. The desperate myth that Algeria was the southern portion of France tore the French nation apart in the 1950s, created the crisis which brought Charles de Gaulle into power in 1958, and maintained tensions between the Right and the Left in France until Algeria's independence in 1962, with an additional aftermath of bitterness in the trail of the career of Charles de Gaulle.

This effect of trying to maintain Algeria as the southern portion of a major European nation had taken place at a time when in other respects North Africa had become substantially an extension of Asia. From the seventh century onwards the gradual Islamization and Arabization of North Africa helped to prepare the ground for converting North Africa's links more firmly in the direction of West Asia, without necessarily ending residual interaction with South Europe. The Arabs themselves had become a bi-continental people, traversing both Africa and Asia. The majority of the Arab people by the twentieth century

[2] See R. R. Palmer in collaboration with Joel Colton, *A History of the Modern World* (New York: Knopf, 1962), 2nd edn, p. 13.

[3] See Herskovits' contribution to Wellesley College, *Symposium on Africa* (Wellesley College, Massachusetts, 1960), p. 16.

were in fact within the African continent, though the majority of Arab states by the last quarter of the twentieth century were in West Asia.

The Arabic language has many more speakers in the African continent than in the Arabian peninsula. And Arabic itself has become the most important single language in the African continent in terms of number of speakers.

An additional factor which has provided linkages between Africa and Asia is the role of Islam. As we shall indicate later, Islam is in distribution basically an Afro-Asian religion since virtually all Muslim nations are either in Africa or in Asia. But we shall also indicate how Christianity is, in distribution, an Afro-Western religion, since almost all Christian nations are either part of the West or part of Africa. Once again, in terms of the history of religion, Africa has been central enough to be a particularly suitable arena for a spirit of ecumenicalism between Islam and Christianity.

In the politics of the Third World Africa also has credentials for being considered central. The Third World is basically tri-continental with Latin America to the West, Asia to the East, and Africa in the middle. The bonds between Africa and Asia include the experience of racial humiliation as non-white people. The bonds between Africa and Latin America include the experience of exploitation. Latin America is to the United States what Africa has been to western Europe, an arena of penetration and control by a colossus of the North.

There are other links and similarities between Africa and Latin America. There is the burden of fragmentation in Latin America comparable to that in Africa, though not as acute. Both continents are split up into competitive countries, some of them tiny, and both are vulnerable to external exploitation as a result.

Both continents have one member dramatically larger than any other: Latin America has its Brazil, Africa has its Nigeria.

Both continents have their comparable mineral resources, providing grounds for competition, but often also providing grounds for consultation and collaboration. These include not only oil but also copper which often brings together countries like Zambia, Zaire and Chile.

Both continents have comparable agricultural economies, once again sometimes creating competition and at other times collaboration. When it comes to coffee production, there are reasons for intense consultation between Brazil on one side and such African coffee producers as Kenya, Uganda and the Ivory Coast on the other.

Then there is the black factor in the racial composition of Latin America, with special reference to countries like Brazil and Cuba. In the case of Africa's relations with Cuba, this black factor in Cuba's composition as a nation has already been of some relevance in lending legitimacy to Cuba's involvement in African affairs. The government in Havana has often emphasized that Cuba is ultimately "an Afro-Latin country". Black Cuban troops engaged in African wars have helped to reduce the image of foreignness in Cuba's intervention.

Also as a link between Africa and Latin America in the future may well be the Portuguese language. Brazil is to Portugal what the United States is to Britain: a child that grew too large for the mother. And just as the United States will in time overshadow Great Britain in influence in former British colonies in Africa, so Brazil will one day overshadow Portugal in influence in former Portuguese colonies in Africa.

There is also another link between Africa and Latin America, a major historical link which is perhaps underestimated. I myself believe that the Monroe Doctrine, that the United States proclaimed in order to keep Europeans out of Latin America, helped to seal the colonial fate of Africa in the decades which followed. The Monroe Doctrine was contained in a message to the Congress of the United States on 2 December 1823. The situation which provoked the message was the threat of European intervention in the Spanish American colonies which were at the time in revolt. The threat amounted to the possibility of a European recolonization of Latin America.

The Monroe Doctrine stipulated that the American hemisphere was no territory for future European colonization, that the United States would regard any attempt by European powers to penetrate the Americas afresh as dangerous to the peace and security of the United States. But it added that the United States would not interfere with European colonies already established in the hemisphere, nor would the United States participate in purely European wars.

The question which I am raising is whether the decision by the United States to insulate Latin America from European recolonization helped to divert European imperialism more firmly towards Africa. After all, the Americans took the Monroe Doctrine quite seriously. It was applied in 1867 to force the withdrawal of French troops from Mexico after the French had established Emperor Maximilian. And in 1895 the United States brought pressure to bear on Great Britain to settle the boundary between British Guyana and Venezuela by arbitration.

If Latin America in the wake of Spain's decline had been available for recolonization by other European powers, the scramble for the African continent might have been delayed. Moreover, it is conceivable that a smaller portion of Africa would have been colonized if the European powers had been busy with new colonial and neo-colonial possessions in Latin America. After all, Africa was at the time a much less attractive proposition, partly because so little was known about it. It was less developed than Latin America, less accessible to outsiders, less evaluated in economic and strategic terms. Putting a French emperor in Mexico seemed by far a more attractive proposition than sending a conquering expedition to the mouth of the Senegal River or the meandering torrents of the River Congo.

My second hypothesis is that the Monroe Doctrine, having preserved Latin America for American influence, helped to keep the United States from the scramble for the African continent later in the century. After all, the United States was already a major power (though not yet a superpower) in the last decades of the nineteenth century. It was represented at the Berlin Congress of 1884-5 where the rules of the scramble for and partition of Africa were tentatively discussed and worked out. But American imperialism decided to concentrate on potential acquisitions closer to home. To this extent the Monroe Doctrine was combined with the slogan "Manifest Destiny". This was a phrase used by Americans in the middle of the nineteenth century to legitimize territorial expansion. Its origins have been traced to an unsigned article in *The United States Magazine and Democratic Review* of July 1845. The article referred to "the fulfillment of our Manifest Destiny to overspread the continent allotted by Providence for the free development of our yearly multiplying millions". The phrase soon became popular with expansionist members of Congress, anxious for war with Mexico in order to acquire more territory, and hungry for the acquisition of California. Thus the Monroe Doctrine allowed the United States greater leverage for indirect imperialism in, or exercised over, Latin America, and the Manifest Destiny slogan allowed the United States to indulge in the more direct imperialism of annexing contiguous territory into its own body politic. By the Treaty of Guadeloupe Hidalgo (February 1848) Mexico ceded to the United States New Mexico and California, where incidentally, or not so incidentally, gold had just been discovered. Mexico also renounced all claims to Texas and recognized the Rio Grande frontier.

The question which arises is whether these imperialist activities by the United States in its own hemisphere were at least a contributory factor towards the absence of American colonies in Africa, apart from the special case of Liberia as a home for returning black Americans. Without the special hemispheric preoccupations which kept the United States busy in Latin America and in expanding its own body politic, it is quite conceivable that the Star-Spangled Banner would indeed have been flying somewhere between the shores of Tripoli and the snows of Kilimanjaro, or somewhere between the mouth of the Volta River and the storms of the Cape of Good Hope.

In this sense, Latin America played a part in neutralizing the United States as a potential imperial power within the African continent. On the other hand, Latin America, by being insulated from European recolonization, helped force the Europeans even earlier to look to Africa for new worlds to conquer. It is partly these historical issues which help to convert Africa into the middle continent of the Third World. Black Africa, as we indicated, provides an important link with Latin America; Arab Africa in the north provides an important link with Asia. But both parts of Africa, north and south of the Sahara, have had links with other sides of the Third World in any case, and have continued to consolidate Africa as the middle continent in the Thid World movement.

In the 1970s Afro-Asianism was strengthened mainly through the Arab connection and the rise of oil power. Afro-Latinism was also strengthened, mainly through the Cuban connection, especially Cuba's participation in the liberation of Angola.

As for the changing identity of North Africa, it is now no longer deemed the southern portion of Europe, but it is sometimes regarded as the western extension of West Asia. Indeed, the very name "The Maghreb" means "the West" in that sense.

But simultaneously with being an extension of West Asia, North Africa remains of course part of Africa. The centrality of the African continent with regard to the three ancient continents is captured precisely in this fluctuating identity of the northern portion of Africa.

Africa's strategic position has provided other areas of linkage. For example, the politics of who controls the Red Sea have bedevilled diplomacy and politics in the Horn of Africa. Competition between the West and the Soviet Union in influencing Somalia and Ethiopia has in part been a debate about how ideologically "red" the Red Sea should be. And if the Soviet Union did effectively control the mouth of the Red Sea and the Gulf of Aden, how imperilled would western oil routes become?

The struggle in Eritrea is also partly an agony of strategic considerations. This is a region astride the Red Sea, and unwillingly incorporated into the body politic of Ethiopia. Would independence for Eritrea convert the Red Sea into an Arab lake? And would this pose a serious danger to an important outlet for Israel in spite of Israel's peace treaty with Egypt?

On balance Africa's location is pregnant with implications for much of the trade and traffic of the world and for many of the minerals and other resources that the rest of the world needs.

And yet in spite of this centrality of location physically and in terms of political economy, Africa is marginal in influence and power within the global system. What are the causes of this marginality? And can the marginality be transcended?

In these six brief lectures I seek to confront this African condition in its totality, knowing full well that the subject matter is not only too big for six lectures but too great for any one lecturer.

But the African condition is in any case in the eye of the beholder. Given that I am a student of politics I shall be particularly susceptible to political nuances in a given situation. Africa looms large to me in its political dimensions.

But even politically, how should I organise the mass of material which confronts me? It is fortunate that there are six Reith lectures, for I propose to address myself to six fundamental paradoxes of the African predicament.

The first is *the paradox of habitation*. Africa is the earliest habitat of man, but is in a sense the last to become truly habitable.

Secondly, we have the paradox of humiliation. Africans are not necessarily the most brutalized of peoples, but they are almost certainly the most humiliated in modern history.

Thirdly, there is *the paradox of acculturation*. African societies are not the closest culturally to the western world, but they have been undergoing the most rapid pace of westernization witnessed this century.

Fourthly, we have *the paradox of fragmentation*. Africa is by no means the smallest of the continents physically, but it is almost definitely the most fragmented politically.

Fifthly, we must bear witness to *the paradox of retardation*. Africa is not the poorest of the regions of the world, but after Antarctica it may well be technically the most retarded and least developed.

And finally we return to *the basic paradox of location*. Africa is the most centrally located of all continents on the globe physically, but again after Antarctica it is probably the most peripheral politically.

In these lectures I hope to address myself to these six paradoxes of Africa's predicament as an underdeveloped continent.

My initial thanks are to the British Broadcasting Corporation itself for giving me this distinguished platform from which to address millions of people on these issues of importance to the peoples of Africa. The BBC was generous with travel funds which enabled me to visit a number of African countries on two separate trips. Funds were set aside for other trips if I needed them. It was a measure of how seriously the Corporation took this special assignment on Africa as it enters the 1980s.

On the trips I made to African countries for these lectures, I was privileged to interview two reigning presidents (one English-speaking and the other French-speaking), one former president, the Secretary-General of the Organization of African Unity, the Administrative Secretary or Head of the United Nations Commission for Africa, officials of the African Development Bank, officials and consultants of UNESCO, officials of the All-Africa Conference of Churches, select officials of other international organizations, select ambassadors of African and western governments, a variety of different journalists and of course fellow scholars and intellectuals in three continents. My benefactors are too numerous to be thanked individually, but these lectures would have been thinner in substance and narrower in scope without their stimulation.

A special role was assumed by Mr Michael Green, my BBC producer for these lectures. He travelled with me in West Africa and came to work with me in Michigan on the drafts of the lectures. Michael is exceptionally gifted in manipulating the potentialities of radio broadcasting to the best advantage. His task was principally to ensure that I approximated that delicate balance between scholarship and argument, between academic quality and popular intelligibility. But in fact Mr Green's value for me turned out to be much greater than merely as a consultant on balance. He is a novice on African affairs, but he turned that shortcoming into a great asset. He challenged me to explain my positions to him, defend them, elaborate on them. In asking me to explain issues to him, he was in fact forcing me to clarify matters to myself more fully.

To Michael Green's persistent and carefully orchestrated intellectual challenges, these lectures owe more than their author can adequately express.

The Center for Afroamerican and African Studies (CAAS) at the University of Michigan provided the basic local support in the preparation of these lectures. I am indebted to my colleagues Professors Niara Sudarkasa and Godfrey Uzoigwe for relieving me of some of my administrative duties as Director of CAAS to enable me to meet the demands of preparing these lectures within a carefully planned timetable. Ms. Rosellen Cheek, my Administrative Assistant at CAAS, also undertook additional burdens during this period with characteristic competence.

Dr Henry D'Souza of Kenyatta University College, Nairobi, was of great help in some of the preliminary research for these lectures.

The typing of the different drafts of the lectures fell upon my inwardly committed and outwardly unflappable Secretary, Mrs Valerie Ward, assisted by Mrs Catherine Coury and Ms. Emily Palmer. Without their teamwork the 1979 Reith Lectures would have found it much harder to meet the carefully programmed deadlines.

To my Chairman of the Department of Political Science at Michigan I am grateful for a re-scheduling of my teaching responsibilities to suit the timetable for the Reith Lectures.

The initial audience of the Reith Lectures was always intended to be British. But I have a British audience all the time in my home — my Yorkshire wife, Molly. She prepared me well for the honour that these lectures have bestowed upon me.

The lectures published in this written form are not identical with those which were delivered on the radio. This medium of the written word has given me room for greater elaboration and more detailed analysis.

A.A.M

1979

LECTURE 1

A Garden of Eden in Decay

In the Reith Lectures of 1962 Dame Margery Perham, the Oxford Historian, decided to use a metaphor from accounting. Her lectures were a "Colonial Reckoning", a kind of balance sheet of the costs and benefits of the colonial experience for both the colonized and the imperial powers.

My own metaphor for these Reith Lectures is from the medical field. It is as if I were a doctor and Africa came to me and asked for a comprehensive medical examination on the eve of a particular anniversary. The most important century in Africa's relations with Europe is the century from the 1880s to the 1980s. It was in the 1880s that the Conference of Berlin was held to agree on the terms of the European partition of Africa. It was in the 1880s that Egypt was occupied, that the Nile Valley was scrambled for, and that the repercussions for the rest of the continent were released. It was in the 1880s that the map of Africa began to acquire more decisively the different flag colours of the occupation powers of Europe. Let us assume Africa has come to my clinic for varied medical tests on the eve of the hundredth anniversary of Europe's rape of her body and her possessions.

We have therefore entitled this series of lectures "The African Condition" for two major reasons. One reason is diagnostic. To some extent this series is about Africa's aches and pains. The Reith Lectures are hereby converting themselves into such devices as a thermometer to estimate the temperature of Africa's body politic. Is something seriously wrong? If so, what is it?

What is Africa's state of health after a hundred years of intense interaction with Europe?

But the title of this year's Reith Lectures was also chosen because it echoed the philosophical phrase "the human condition". We propose to examine the state of Africa partly as a way of measuring the state of the world. Africa is in part a mirror of the human condition.

But in a mirror the left hand becomes the right hand and vice versa. The mirror is both a reflection of reality and its distortion. The mirror is a paradox.

My approach in these lectures will exploit paradox as a mode of analysis. Platonists, Hegelians and Marxists also use paradox as a tool for studying reality, but they call it the "dialectic". Qualities which are seemingly contradictory are reconciled. Reality is always a unit of opposites.

We have chosen to focus on six paradoxes of the African condition in these lectures. One is the paradox of the Garden of Eden in decay. Africa is probably the first home of mankind, but it is the last to be made truly habitable. The Garden of Eden is partly barren, a victim of soil erosion and decay. On the other hand, the garden is in part overgrown, a victim of human neglect. My first lecture today will turn to this paradox, after this general introduction to the series as a whole.

In my second lecture I shall address myself to the paradox of an Africa humiliated but not brutalized. The television series "Roots" in the United States was followed by the series "Holocaust". "Roots" is a story of black humiliation from slavery to present-day racism. "Holocaust" is a story of the brutalization of the Jews. Among victims of sheer physical brutality, blacks are not necessarily the worst sufferers. The Jews can match that martyrdom. But among victims of sheer humiliation and contempt, Africans and people of African ancestry have suffered the most in modern history.

My third paradox concerns a clash of cultures, a cult of acculturation. African societies are not the closest culturally to the western world, but they have been experiencing what is perhaps the most rapid pace of westernization witnessed this century. The continent is controlled disproportionately by westernized Africans. European languages are relentlessly on the rampage in the continent, destroying or undermining one local culture after another. Africans are caught up between rebellion against the West and imitation of the West.

In my fourth lecture my terms of reference will be the burden of Africa's underdevelopment itself. A continent rich in resources is poor in performance. A well-endowed region of the world accommodates what the United Nations regards as the poorest countries in the world. Why this paradox of poverty-stricken millions in the golden continent? For goodness' sake, why?

Then we have the paradox of a continent large enough to be Jonathan Swift's Brobdingnag, but inhabited by minute Lilliputians. Among the continents of the world, Africa is second only to Asia in size, but it is fragmented into more than four dozen little Lilliputs. I shall be handling this dialectic of fragmentation in my fifth lecture.

My final lecture will look at Africa's physical location on the globe in relation to its economic, political and military destiny. Physically, Africa is the most central of all continents in geographical location, but politically and militarily it is probably the most marginal. What are the implications of this paradox of being physically central but strategically and politically peripheral and weak? And how is Africa to get out of the prison-house of political dwarfs situated in the middle of the City of Man?

If you have a world map or a globe in your sitting room you may like to consult it in connection with some of these observations.

With regard to the size of the different continents, it is quite amazing how far European ethnocentrism has influenced cartographic projections over the centuries. The northern hemisphere continues to loom disproportionately large in the great majority of atlases to the present day. Of course the distortion of the north goes back to the days when cartography involved very few measurements and very little of what we would today call "the scientific method". But the legacy of Gerhardus Mercator, the greatest of the sixteenth-century European cartographers, has continued to distort size on the map in favour of the northern continents of the world. If you look at a modern map based on the Mercator projection North America appears to be one and a half times the size of Africa. On a Mercator projection it is difficult to believe that, on the contrary, Africa is three and a half times the size of the United States.

The Briesemeister projection of more recent times attempts to give an elliptical equal-area focus, presenting the different continents in relation to square miles. Visually, Africa emerges as the second largest of the inhabited continents, trailing behind only Asia.

On the Mercator projection Greenland seems to be almost in competition with Africa in size, which is of course preposterous, since Greenland is only a fraction of Africa's size in square miles.

In the course of the North—South dialogue in Paris in 1977 concerning the new international economic order the issue of distortion of images came up. Maps were displayed, some showing the legacy of the Mercator projection with its strong tendency to exaggerate the size of the northern hemisphere, others with new projections which try more systematically to relate the sizes of continents on a flat map to the sizes they would be on a tiny globe, thus achieving greater approximation to the actual number of square miles per continent. The visual memories of millions of children across generations have carried distorted ideas about the comparative physical scale of northern continents in relation to southern ones.

I was myself in Paris in July 1979 at UNESCO headquarters. Subjects discussed at the meetings I attended included a new UNESCO project on the history of human civilizations, which was to update an earlier project. We also discussed a separate project on the history of Africa from the days of the Egyptian pharaohs to the present. At one of the meetings maps were again displayed to show the northern ethnocentrism of the history of cartography in the West. In private discussions there were speculations about the impact of these distortions on western self-images, and the repercussions of these self-images in the West's relations with the peoples of the southern continent. Indeed, most maps used in African schools disproportionately invoke the Mercator projection in portraying the world.

The Armadillo projection of the world is a compromise between the Mercator and the Briesemeister projections. It seeks on the one hand to minimize the distortions in size inherent in the Mercator version, and on the other, to maintain on a flat page the image of what a map drawn on the shell of an armadillo when he is rolled up like a ball would look like when he unrolls.

What is of course clear is that Africa is a continent larger in square miles than China and India added together, and capable of absorbing several times over the acreage of all the imperial powers that have ravished or conquered her throughout the centuries.

The distortions of representations of the size of the continent arose partly out of the decision of cartographers to equate the north of the world with the top of the world. Neither on the rounded globe nor on the flattened map is it scientifically necessary that Europe should be above Africa. On the whole, the decision to make the Arctic Ocean "up" and Antarctica "down" was an accident in the history of science rather than the logic of the cosmos. We like to think of our globe revolving in the Milky Way with Greenland at the top instead of at the bottom. But if we could imagine ourselves to be spectators from the opposite side of the globe, we might have to readjust our deeply ingrained images of "up" and "down" as the equivalent of north and south.

In historical terms the northern hemisphere in the last five hundred years has indeed moved up in terms of scientific skills and technological know-how. The North has also been "up" in terms of the Industrial Revolution and the economic pre-eminence it was bestowed upon the countries of Europe and North America. The North has above all been "up" politically in the last two hundred years as it has conquered much of the world, and has maintained control over much of it to the present day. These senses of "up" are real. But in the carthographic sense, of the European continent being "up" and the African continent "down", we are talking about conventions of science rather than dimensions of reality, accidents of map-drawing rather than dictates of the universe.

Africans have often complained about how different branches of knowledge that developed in the western world have over time attempted to scale down everything African, sometimes consciously and at other times subconsciously. Biologists, physical anthropologists and psychologists have periodically debated whether intelligence is a matter of genes, and if so, whether it is racially and ethnically relative. Many have concluded that black people are genetically less intelligent than white ones.

Historians in the West have over a period of time attempted to scale down the importance of the history of African societies.

The most notorious example recently continues to be the assertion of Sir Hugh Trevor-Roper, the Regius Professor of Modern History at Oxford University: "Maybe in the future there will be some African history, but at the moment there is none. . . . There is only the history of Europeans in Africa. . . . The rest is darkness, and darkness is not a subject of history."[1]

Social and cultural anthropologists have scaled down African structures and cultures, though often with affection and possessiveness. Western anthropological scholars have "adopted" different African "tribes", studying them as special cases of "primitive societies". There has already been an African rebellion against anthropological lapses in the West, and major changes have taken place in western anthropology more consistent nor only with the dignity of African peoples but, at least as important, with genuinely scientific commitment.

But what is only just being tackled now is the distortion of the geographer, the ethnocentrism of the western cartographer. Africa might have been denied its full credentials as a part of human civilization, but must it also be denied its size in square miles? Can we not begin to experiment in schools with maps and globes that are less distorting? Should we not include in every school atlas the alternative scenario of "turning the world the other side up", with South America at the top and North America below, with Africa above and Europe beneath? Should not all geography lessons be more explicit about the danger of ethnocentrism even in map-making?

Karl Marx attempted to put Hegel the right side up, restoring the primacy of material conditions over ideas. Future mapmakers may need to put the globe the right side up, restoring a much needed status to the cradle of mankind, Africa, where human history first began.

This brings us back to the paradox of the Garden of Eden in decay. This earliest home of man has a crisis of habitability. Many parts of it are not yet fit for human habitation.

I would like to divide minimum liveable conditions into three kinds. To begin with, there are *the ecological conditions* such as climate and the nature of the terrain. How suitable for relatively comfortable human life is the physical environment in Africa?

---

[1] Hugh Trevor-Roper, "The Rise of Christian Europe", *The Listener* (London), 28 November 1963, p. 871. For a response, see J. D. Fage, *On the Nature of African History* (Inaugural lecture, University of Birmingham, March 1965).

Then there are *the technical conditions* of habitation, with special reference to minimum technological mastery over nature. How easily available are the technological skills of survival in Africa?

Thirdly, there are *the socio-political conditions* and the degree to which these make a place congenial to relatively peaceful human existence. Have present-day Africans made such a mess of their social and political arrangements that the place has become *less* suitable for civilized existence since the Europeans tampered with it, rather than more?

In relation to minimum ecological conditions of habitation, the European impact on Africa has been progressive. Europe has not changed Africa's climate, but has enabled Africans to better understand processes such as soil erosion and what is nowadays referred to as "desertification'. Understanding ecology is the first step towards either controlling it or adjusting to it.

Closely related to all this is Europe's impact on the technical conditions for habitation in Africa. Important skills have found their way to Africa by way of the colonial transmission belt. Africa is now better equipped to deal with diseases and to build roads and railways than it was before European penetration and colonization.

The negative impact of Europe has been more on the socio-political conditions of habitation than on the ecological and technical.

Europeans destroyed African institutions of authority and government and have left a major political gap. The rules of living together which prevailed in the pre-colonial period, the values and collective responsibilities of traditional social life, were replaced by artificial norms imported from Europe. One colony after another experimented with such artifices as the Westminster model. Europeans in one colony after another had to distinguish one so-called "tribe" from another, while at the same time forcing them to live within the same national boundaries. One colony after another experienced new class formation without necessarily acquiring the necessary capability for effective conflict resolution.

And in those colonies where ecological conditions were particularly congenial for European habitation, there was an influx of European settlers which set the stage for future conflicts with the indigenous inhabitants, future crises of socio-political habitability.

But first let us briefly address ourselves to some of the residual problems of ecological and technical conditions of life in Africa before we return to the pressures of the social and political environment.

Certainly the struggle to make Africa more habitable would require more progress in the control of diseases such as bilharzia, sleeping sickness, cholera and malaria. As we have indicated, this is part of the brighter side of the colonial penetration and the bequest of the white man. Medical science and technology in the West were so far ahead by the time of the colonization of Africa that it made a difference to the quality of life of at least certain sectors of African societies. Infant mortality fell, however inadequately; life expectancy rose, however modestly. And the population of Africa began to increase noticeably as the death rate fell with improved medication, information and therapy.

The habitability of Africa has also required a capacity to tame nature. Once again western technology was well advanced before the white man arrived in Africa. When he did arrive that technology proceeded to increase production per acre where it suited the white man to increase it; to build roads where it served the white man's interests; to control wild animals where it was prudent or desirable; to build dams and divert rivers; and to penetrate deep into the African soil for minerals. The taming of nature in Africa has of course been spasmodic; partly because nature is so aggressive at times in the tropics. Moreover, there are problems of desertification, — that is, the expanding acreage of barren land. Nature is still playing havoc with Africa's habitability in places like the Sahel. Human beings are also aggravating desertification partly through ignorance concerning soil erosion, and partly through the ruthless self-interest of those who cut down trees for commercial purposes or other kinds of immediate or short-term gain. Famine hits parts of Africa in a big way from time to time, and the international community has yet to find the will or mobilize the means to tame nature in Africa sufficiently well to ensure a relatively stable habitat.

A fourth area which cries out for improvement is opening up the continent to itself by strengthening communications east to west, north to south, and diagonally. Means of transportation and contact in Africa are notoriously rudimentary. In many cases it is easier for one part of Africa to communicate with Europe than with another part of Africa. Certainly telecommunications and air transportation still bear the colonial stamp, which makes them serve Africa's interaction with Europe rather than with itself, It is now possible to dial the United States directly from one's private telephone in Nairobi or Mombasa but it is not possible to dial Lagos or Abidjan from that same telephone.

Ground transportation is simply rudimentary, with limited railway lines even nationally, and vulnerable roadways, subject to vegetation growth and in any case not adequate for extensive penetration into the hinterland.

Many questions still hang over this whole paradox of habitation. Why was this earliest home of man condemned to such a slow pace of technical, ecological and socio-political habitability? Why were communications slower to develop in this continent than in some others? Why did serious diseases last longer? Why did structures of habitation, homes for families, remain so modest south of the Sahara? And what did all this have to do with the influx of white men from outside, seeking new lands to conquer, new wealth to acquire, new areas to inhabit?

One of the last acts of Africa's political crisis of habitation is being played out in southern Africa. White immigrants penetrated that portion of the continent, tilling the land, extracting the minerals, constructing new homes for themselves and for others, while at the same time containing and controlling an older wave of migrants, the blacks.

In this lecture we shall not linger too long on the first part of the paradox, that Africa is probably man's first home. We are concentrating on the second portion of the paradox, that Africa has been slow to become truly habitable.

Nevertheless, it is worth at least recognizing that recent archaeological discoveries increase the probability that if there was a Garden of Eden where the first man and woman lived, that garden was probably located in the African continent. It was not a case of Eve being created out of Adam's rib; it was more a case of both Adam and Eve being created out of the loins of an older species. An important breakthrough was the classical discovery made by Louis Leakey of Kenya, the discovery of the *Proconsul* within the ape line, with the brain larger and the eyes more clearly focused in stereoscopic vision. The name *Proconsul* for this specimen was an exercise in anthropological wit. The name was intended to suggest that Leakey's find was a forebear of a famous chimpanzee at the London Zoo in 1931 whose nickname was Consul.

The increasing evidence that man first became man in Africa has provided ammunition both to racists and to African nationalists. The racists attempted to take us back to social Darwinism and the old theory of the "great chain of being".

The old theory was static and was based on the ancient idea that God had so organized the world that the universe and creation were arranged in a great chain of being; that all creatures could be classified and fitted into a hierarchy extending "from man down to the smallest reptile, whose existence can be discovered by the microscope".[2]

But it was not just the species which were so classified. Even within the highest species (that of human beings) there were in turn divisions. The theory of the great chain of being assumed that the Almighty in His wisdom did not want a big gap between one type of creature and the next. So there had to be intermediate categories between orang-utans and white men. As early as 1713 naturalists began looking for the "missing link" between men and apes and apparently speculated on the possibility that the Hottentots of South Africa and orang-utans might be side by side in the "scale of life", separated only by the fact that orang-utans could not speak.[3]

To the racists it is not surprising that archaeologists should discover the missing link between man and ape in Africa. Many white settlers in the African continent still regard Africans as having only recently landed on the ground from the trees, only one incarnation after the monkey.

Newspapers and public speeches in southern Africa are now less likely than they were a couple of decades ago to express the

[2] Charles White, *An Account of the Regular Graduations in Man* (London, 1799), Vol. I.   Consult also A. O. Lovejoy, *The Great Chain of Being* (Cambridge, Mass., 1936).

[3] Lovejoy, ibid., pp. 233ff.; also Lovejoy, "Some Eighteenth Century Evolutionists", *Popular Science Monthly* (1904), Vol. LXV, p. 327.

more blatant neo-Darwinism equating blacks with the missing link between apes and human beings, but ideas of this kind persist at the subconscious level. And much of the insistence on racial segregation in the relations between white people and black people in Africa has been due to a deeply ingrained superstition that blacks are a different and lower species.

In African nationalism and romantic thought, on the other hand, the discovery that Africa may be man's first home touches a chord of pride. The archaeologists provide ammunition for those who would insist that Africa is the original Garden of Eden. This particular view of the nature of original Africa links up with ideas about the age of innocence in Africa well before Europe desecrated the holy kingdom.

One important school of romantic thought in modern Africa goes under the name of "Negritude". Suffice it to note for the time being what an English colleague and I had occasion to observe in a joint article several years ago:

> Negritude is apt to drift into an exaggerated portrayal of traditional precolonial Africa as a Garden of Eden. Perhaps this is part of a larger phenomenon. Perhaps it is a curious aspect of the planting of Christianity itself in Africa that there is an absence of conviction that man before the invention of colonialism was ever evil.[4]

The mood of this branch of African romantic thought is one of nostalgia, yearning for an innocence which is eternally lost. All that can be done now is to make the best of a bad job, try to save some of the values of old Africa, and find a synthesis between these and the influences which have come with colonialism and modernity.

But, thanks to the archaeologists, there are occasions when the Garden of Eden in Africa is literal rather than metaphorical. There is a belief that Adam was a black man, a theme which seems to be shared by black American Muslims in the United States. Scientific knowledge available today may conceivably be on the side of the black Muslim theology of the late Elijah Muhammad in America. It is not certain that the first man was black but, as we have noted, there seems to be increasing

---

[4] Mazrui and G. F. Engholm, "Rousseau and Intellectualized Populism in Africa", *The Review of Politics* (U.S.A.) (January 1968), Vol. 30, No. 1, p. 24.

evidence to vindicate the claim that the first man was African. The eastern seaboard of the continent, my own cradle as an individual, might well turn out to be the cradle of mankind as a whole. The Garden of Eden as a symbol of the birth of humanity and the Garden of Eden as a symbol of the moment of absolute innocence converge in the romantic ideas of significant sections of black peoples.

Of course negritude and other schools of African romantic thought have their African critics as well as their converts. Ezekiel Mphahlele, the South African writer, was among the earliest black rebels against the pristine assumptions of negritude. Mphahlele believes that when negritude assumes too much innocence it cannot at the same time attribute to African man the capacity for natural spontaneity. After all, to be spontaneous sometimes implies reacting in violent ways. At a conference in Dakar in April 1963 Mphahlele explosively said:

> I do not accept . . . the way in which too much of the poetry inspired by Negritude romanticises Africa — as a symbol of innocence, purity and artless primitiveness. I feel insulted when some people imply that Africa is not also a violent continent. I am a violent person, and proud of it because it is often a healthy state of mind.[5]

By putting an extra emphasis on African violence Ezekiel Mphahlele was touching upon the second part of our paradox of habitation — the slow pace by which Africa has become socially and politically habitable. In a brilliant hyperbole Mphahlele shocked some of his negritudist listerners at the same meeting:

> Some day I'm going to plunder, rape, set things on fire; I am going to cut someone's throat; I am going to subvert the government; I am going to organise a coup d'etat; yes, I am going to oppose my own peoples; I am going to hunt down the rich fat black men who bully the small weak black men and destroy them; I am going to become a capitalist, and woe to all those who cross my path or who want to be my servants or chauffeurs and so on; I am going to lead a breakaway church — there is money in it;

[5] "Negritude and its Enemies: A Reply", in Gerald Moore (ed.), *African Literature and the Universities* (Ibadan: Ibadan University Press, 1965), p. 25.

I am going to attack the black bourgeoisie while I cultivate a garden, rear dogs and parrots; listen to jazz and classics, read "culture" and so on. Yes, I am also going to organise a strike. Don't you know that sometimes I kill to the rhythm of drums and cut the sinews of a baby to cure it of paralysis?[6]

In fact Mphahlele remains one of the least violent human beings I've ever met. But as a black South African in exile he witnessed the crisis of habitation in black Africa. A distinguished writer though he was, he nevertheless suffered the economic suspicions and political distrust that so many refugees in Africa have to confront from their own fellow Africans. He lived and worked in Zambia, Nigeria and Kenya. He left Africa somewhat disenchanted, convinced that there was indeed a crisis of habitability at least for African emigres.

After teaching for a while in the United States, Mphahlele decided to go back to white-dominated South Africa itself. Politically and socially the conditions of habitation were oppressive for non-white people in Mphahlele's own land. But he was one South African exile who decided it was time to go home — and suffer with the people. He had decided to come to terms with Africa's paradox of habitation.

But for millions of others a simmering unease continues. Black Africa has one of the largest refugee problems in the world, alongside south-east Asia. Over a third of the total number of refugees in the world may be in black Africa, depending upon how one defines a refugee. Many Africans have fled from their homes as a result of tyrannical governments such as those of Guinea (Conakry) until recently; Uganda until the overthrow of Idi Amin; and Ethiopia since the revolution which overthrew Emperor Haile Selassie. But other refugees have fled not merely because their governments were tyrannical but because of deep and seemingly irreconcilable ethnic cleavages in their own societies. These include the thousands of refugees from Rwanda and Burundi, as well as thousands from countries like Zaïre, Angola and Uganda during and after Idi Amin. All this is quite apart from the vast numbers that have been running away either from racial domination or racial warfare in Zimbabwe, Namibia and South Africa.

[6] Ezekiel Mphahlele, *The African Image* (New York: Frederick A. Praeger, 1962), p. 23.

There is less drama in Africa about refugees than there has been in places like south-east Asia and the Indian subcontinent. This is partly because African refugees do not take to international waters in a high drama of "Give me liberty or give me death beneath the seas". Crossing a land border while running away from domestic butchery is more mundane. But in addition, the African refugee problem is less visible because some of the African countries concerned are themselves small and may have small populations. The number of refugees is very large indeed when all are added together, but the numbers of those running away from specific countries are modest compared with numbers in Asia. Thus little Equatorial Guinea had one-third of its population in exile, but it was a tiny country in West Africa, formerly a French colony, and later inherited by a particularly brutal black dictator. The continent of Africa contains less than five hundred million people, divided among fifty countries. That is less then ten million people per country on the average.

But when you add the number of refugees together, the problem becomes larger *per capita* than anywhere else in the world apart from that of the Palestinian diaspora. The crisis of political habitability continues to haunt the African continent. Migration of people is a great measurement of habitability. Refugees are often people voting with their feet, a mobile referendum on the march.

But perhaps of greater international implications is African migration to the developed industrial countries, especially the western world. Some western countries are tightening up their immigration requirements; others are liberalizing. On the whole, the United States has become more liberal. The present situation is a far cry from the law which was adopted in 1921 imposing a quota system for immigration based on national origins. This law limited the number of immigrants to about fifty-four thousand per year, to be distributed among countries of origin in proportion to what those countries had already contributed to the composition of the American population at that time. This meant that the United Kingdom got the highest priority, followed by other European countries. (For Latin American, Canadian and Caribbean immigrants the United States adopted different legislation.)

This quota system of immigration based on ethnic and

national origins has now been abolished by the American Congress. One result has been a dramatic rise of immigration into America from Asia and, to a much lesser extent, Africa. Asians and Africans now stand a better chance to being allowed to settle in the United States than they did under the quota system of 1921.

As I have indicated to both American and African audiences, we may be witnessing the most significant wave of African migration to the Americas since the end of the slave trade. I have argued that this might even be the first really *voluntary* wave of African migration westward across the Atlantic ever.

> The migrants will not be helpless captives from African villages, rustic and bewildered, but will be some of the most sophisticated Africans in history. The brain drain from Africa will be gathering momentum in the 1980s. The migrants will be either seeking refuge from anti-intellectual dictatorial rulers or will be seeking new economic or academic opportunities for themselves. They will be inspired by the same range of general motives as migrants from other lands since the *Mayflower*.[7]

These migrants are what might be called the black Pilgrim Fathers, running away from the crisis of political habitation in Africa.

Since I decided to run away from Amin's Uganda I myself have joined this group. I have become part of what is now known as the *brain drain*.

Like so many other émigrés, many of us have guilt complexes about being away from home. Many of us are eager to reassure our friends that we regard our sojourn in the West as decidedly temporary.

But should we feel guilty at all? Are we not merely symptoms of Africa's paradox of habitation and crisis of habitability? In any case, is there not something to be said in favour of such exile?

I once attempted to make a case precisely for my kind of exile to readers of my Sunday column in a newspaper in my own country, Kenya. Nothing I have ever written for a news-

[7]Mazrui, *Political Values and the Educated Class in Africa* (London: Heinemann Educational Books; Berkeley and Los Angeles: University of California Press, 1978), p. 375.

paper has ever provoked such instantaneous and militant indignation. Some of the letters from readers of the *Sunday Nation* in Nairobi were so abusive that the editor, having published them, felt constrained to write to me and virtually apologize for the tone of some of the letters.

Yet the points I was making were relatively obvious. Africa has for too long been penetrated by others without attempting to counter-penetrate in return. Our continent has over the centuries been invaded from outside by foreign travellers, traders, slave dealers, explorers, missionaries, colonizers and teachers. We have for too long been passive receivers rather than active interventionists.

I cannot help feeling that it is about time Africa sent missionaries to Europe and America, as well as teachers, engineers, doctors and ordinary workers. Perhaps one day Africa might even be able to send black mercenaries to interfer in a civil war in Ireland or Quebec.

It is indeed time that Africa counter-penetrated the western world. A modest beginning has just been made. Westerners in my home town of Mombasa moulded my young mind. They included a Scottish teacher of literature, a tall English military officer who spoke fluent Urdu from his old days as part of the British Raj and who in Kenya decided to adopt me as a protégé, another British officer called Commander Hollebone who criticized the flamboyant colours of my youthful dress and made me self-conscious about my clothes for decades to come, a Dutch manager of a multinational corporation who tried in vain to inculcate in me Dutch managerial efficiency, and a variety of other western personnel who helped to shape the mind of one more young African. Should I feel guilty as I seek to influence young minds at such places as the University of Michigan, or the University of Leeds, or by addressing schoolchildren or young adults in Sweden, Australia and Canada? If westerners have for so long presumed to teach our young and mould their minds, is it not time that Africans began to reverse the process? Is the brain drain only a curse? Or does it have a side that is a blessing?

In any case, it may sometimes be arrogant to criticize the jet set of Africa who migrate to industrialized countries without also criticizing the passengers on the mammy buses who migrate for proletarian jobs in neighbouring African countries. The mammy-crowd or the bus set are those ordinary compatriots who seek to improve their economic fortunes by moving from, say, Tanzania to Kenya, or Upper Volta to the Ivory Coast. Quite often these brothers and sisters cannot afford to buy a ticket on a plane and go to Europe or America, but they can afford to pay a fare for transportation by a bus or the local *Matatu* taxi, packed full. Those who travel by plane to different lands become part of the brain drain. Those who travel by bus or *Matatu* taxi are part of the brain drain. To criticize only the jet set while ignoring labour migration by the *Matatu* crowd is a form of reverse arrogance. It is at least arguable that any double standard in evaluating the jet set as against the *Matatu* crowd is a sign of condescension towards the latter.

Peasants have a right to flee to neighbouring countries when there are atrocities in Burundi or a civil war in Angola. That continues to be part of the crisis of habitability in Africa. Intellectuals should similarly be granted rights where there is tyranny in their own society. Peasants and workers can migrate for jobs across the border; intellectuals have borders that are intercontinental, and should be given occasionally the benefit of the doubt for seeking to improve their lot elsewhere.

And yet, when all is said and done, there is a residual case for at least trying to remain in one's own country if at all possible. The case does rest on issues of loyalty and service. But the burden of responsibility is not merely on those who are tempted to leave. Each African country has also to be fair to its citizens, providing a healthier climate of freedom and opportunity for them. Only such congenial conditions at home in Africa could reduce the volume and scale of the second Bantu migration, set in our own times.

The reasons why Africans migrate are of course varied. Many are abroad for political reasons; more are abroad for reasons of economic ambition. But at times there is also that old-fashioned spirit of adventure which contributed such a lot to Europe's capacity to traverse the world. That spirit seeks new horizons to explore, new worlds to conquer. Europe and the western world have had this spirit for about five hundred years. The spirit produced Christopher Columbus and David Livingstone. It produced conquerors of mountain peaks, explorers of Antarctica, inventors of new machines, and more recently, astronauts and cosmonauts rocketing into outer space.

In a different way, our African ancestors too, the earlier Bantu and Nilotes, had a spirit of curiosity and adventure of their own when they left their villages to traverse and populate an entire continent. Today Africa does not end on its own shores. On the contrary, there is a lot of Africa extending beyond the seas. Some of those Africans abroad were sent to Brazil, the United States or the Caribbean as slaves. Others have gone overseas voluntarily in search of new opportunities, or in quest of greater freedom. To paraphrase an important patriotic English poem:

> Winds of the world give answer,
> They are whimpering to and fro.
>
> And who should know of Africa
> Who only Africa know?

But what about those *non-Africans* who reside within the African continent? What is to be their future?

The answer has varied from one part of the continent to another. At least in the urban areas Kenya has successfully maintained a multiracial society. On the other hand, in Uganda Idi Amin ruthlessly threw out thousands of Asians, and, less directly, made conditions increasingly difficult for all foreigners, as well as for his own people.

But the ultimate question of co-habitation between Africans and non-Africans is of course dramatized in southern Africa. Is the white man in southern Africa truly there to stay? And if he will continue to struggle to ensure that he does stay, to what extremities will he carry his defence? Is the war in Zimbabwe a mere Sunday afternoon picnic as compared with the conflagration in the Republic of South Africa a decade or more later?

Let us first be clear that there has so far been no precedent of any white settler community in Africa, effectively in control of the local situation, giving up power without violence. In every African country which had a sizeable white minority effectively in control, a military challenge was necessary before black majority rule could be introduced. This includes my own country, Kenya, which had to experience the Mau Mau war from 1952 to 1960 before settler control could be broken.

The Algerian war from 1954 to 1962 was another dramatic challenge to white settler power, backed for a while by the establishment in Paris. Angola and Mozambique, in their very different ways, were comparable examples. And now we have the agony of Zimbabwe.

In places where there were no large numbers of white settlers with an infrastructure of control, it was of course easier for the colonial power in Europe to withdraw. Countries like Ghana, Nigeria and Uganda did not have to undergo a sustained war of liberation to convince Britain to pull out. But Algeria, Kenya and the old Rhodesia would never have attained African majority rule without the use of the barrel of the gun by Africans.

This means that the last bastion of white control, the Republic of South Africa, will have to undergo a similar challenge in the years to come. The revolution in South Africa has ultimately to come from within, as the blacks get increasingly radicalized, and their capacity to organize and fight improves. My scenario is approximately as follows. Under international pressure, the Republic of South Africa will increasingly liberalize its system, in fits and starts, two steps forward one step backward. But as a result of that liberalization the opposition to the system will find greater flexibility to organize itself. In time the opposition will include a radical and effectively organized and armed challenge to the white establishment.

The African homelands or Bantustans that the white establishment has created may then have to be recolonized by the whites for security reasons, as acts of sabotage within the white areas increase, and the black homelands serve in part as areas of temporary refuge for guerrillas.

South Africa's neighbours like Mozambique and black-ruled Zimbabwe will also have to brace themselves for Israeli-like reprisals from South Africa if they serve as hosts, unwillingly or willingly, to South African guerrillas. South Africa's neighbours will become the Lebanons of southern Africa: on the one hand, serving as a reluctant host to liberation fighters and guerrillas; and on the other hand, suffering as victims of reprisals from south of the border.

As it happens, the Republic of South Africa and the state of Israel have engaged in extensive consultation concerning their predicament as isolated societies with hostile neighbours. These consultations have included questions of counterinsurgency. The Israelis have been relatively effective in containing the Palestinian threat to their own security. The South African white establishment is interested in learning from Israel's experience.

But more ominous from the point of view of our theme on the crisis of habitability are the reported consultations on cooperation in nuclear research between Israel and the Republic of South Africa. South Africa has the uranium and part of the know-how for the development of a nuclear capability. Israel has more or less the rest of the know-how. Reports about nuclear collaboration between these two international pariahs have alarmed not only Africans, but many friends of Israel. Will Israel's technological expertise enter into an alliance with South Africa's financial power and uranium resources to create parallel nuclear capabilities in the two countries?

I myself am not quite as concerned about South Africa's nuclear capability in the military field as many of my fellow Africans may be. This is because I believe that nuclear power is less relevant for the survival of apartheid than it may be for the survival of the state of Israel. Israel's most dangerous adversaries lie outside Israel, the radical Arab states and the determined Palestinians. But apartheid's most dangerous adversary is within the Republic of South Africa itself, in the form of potential black militancy and radicalism. Israel could conceivably use nuclear weapons against her external adversaries, but the architects of apartheid in South Africa could hardly threaten nuclear annihilation against the restless masses of Soweto. Even if they decided to use tactical nuclear weapons on pockets of insurgents in, say, the Bantustans, such nearness of nuclear pollution would soon begin to send whites themselves tracking to distant lands for refuge. The use of nuclear weapons within the approximate boundaries of the Republic of South Africa is for the time being inconceivable, since it would result in precisely that which the system seeks most to prevent, a large-scale exodus of whites to safer and cleaner air.

But will whites leave South Africa or will they fight to the last proud Afrikaner?

I think there is a lot of foolish romanticism about the Afrikaners. It goes back to the Boer War and even further back to their proud trekking into the hinterland of southern Africa. I agree that Afrikaners have more to lose than English-speaking white South Africans, but I am not persuaded that the majority of them would rather die than seek refuge elsewhere. The majority of any society, any race, any nation, is relatively pragmatic when it comes to issues of life and death. The Afrikaners will fight, they will kill and be killed for a while. But when the cost really becomes too high the exodus will begin.

Nor do I believe the nonsense that circulates from one Africanist party to another to the effect that the Afrikaners or Dutch-speaking white South Africans, have nowhere to go. If there is a revolution in South Africa, and white Afrikaners run out for refuge, I have not the slightest doubt that many western doors will open for them. I cannot imagine the western world shutting its doors against whites on the run from blacks. The Afrikaners will have virtually as much access to the West as the English-speaking South Africans.

The Netherlands may prefer for the time being to maintain a political and moral distance from her sons and daughters in South Africa. But when the racial chips are finally down, and Dutch-speaking whites are on the run from black revolutionaries, Holland will open its doors partly for reasons of kith and kin, and partly for reasons of its own tradition of humanitarianism. The country that permitted thousands of Indonesians and Surinamese to pour into its limited space is unlikely to flinch at admitting its own kith and kin scrambling for safety.

But in any case other western countries too will definitely open their doors, and many Afrikaners will end up in places as distant from each other as New York in North America and Melbourne in Australia, Manchester on one side and Rio de Janeiro on the other.

By that time Africa's crisis of habitability will have hit Africa's last remaining white conquerors, and a large proportion of them will seek more habitable surroundings elsewhere.

And yet I do not expect South Africa to cease being a multiracial society. A third or even half of the total white population may leave when the revolution comes, but a million or two will remain behind to work out an alternative deal with the blacks and attempt to rebuild a fairer society. Later on other whites will re-enter the Republic, if only as businessmen and other kinds of temporary residents. It is conceivable that by the end of the century the proportion of whites within South Africa to blacks will be relatively the same, while power has effectively shifted to the black majority. But half the whites need not be the same people. To illustrate, Kenya today has more white people than there were before black majority rule was conceded. But the proportion of the old style settlers has dramatically declined.

In the ultimate analysis, many white people may continue to find the southern portion of the African continent truly habitable and even pleasant, in spite of the change in political power which is bound to come in the course of the remaining two decades of the twentieth century.

We shall return to some of these problems in subsequent lectures. What is clear is that the long-term solutions to Africa's crisis of habitability lie in Africa's gradual acquisition of two capacities: the capacity for self-pacification and the capacity for self-development. Self-pacification would involve the continent in controlling its own political and social excesses, ranging from tyranny to corruption, from border wars between states to the exploitation of women. We must return to these issues later.

Self-development includes defining goals in relation to available means, and cultivating the will to pursue those goals with as much self-reliance as possible. Excessive dependence on outsiders is part of the imperial malaise, and Africa should seek ways to transcend it.

The Garden of Eden is in disrepair. Much of the natural beauty is still there, some of it lush, some of it rugged. The White Nile finds its way from Lake Victoria towards the Mediterranean, against the background of the Mountains of the Moon of Uganda. The rugged savanna country extends over hundreds of miles elsewhere. The torrents of Victoria Falls pound their way down to eternity. The sand dunes of the Sahara and the Kalahari have their own story of majestic barrenness. Yes, man's first home is still beautiful — but the scars of the original sin are in evidence. *Quo vadis?*

LECTURE 2

The Cross of Humiliation

Our concern in this lecture is with the nature of racial humiliation.

As an African, I have experienced the cross of racial humiliation in person, in a variety of forms, in different countries, at
different stages of my life. After all, I did grow up in a white-
dominated colonial Kenya, and experienced the realities of
day-to-day life in a racially segregated colonial society.

But what I would like to share with you are one or two
experiences I have had as someone married to an English
woman. They are incidents concerning a general social atmosphere, rather than direct victimization.

In the first case, our problem was simply one of not knowing
what to expect when my wife, Molly, and I first visited the
United States together early in 1965. A little while previously
we had been reading in newspapers abroad about the latest
American debate concerning "miscegenation". As late as
the 1960s nearly half the states in the Union had laws against
racially mixed marriages or other forms of sexual mating
across racial lines. In 1963, the United States Supreme Court
had avoided a direct ruling on the constitutionality of laws
which forbade mixed marriages.

And then there we were in Chicago, in 1965, planning to
drive through a number of different states on our way to
Los Angeles. My wife and I were not absolutely sure about
the latest "miscegenation" situation, nor were we certain
whether we would be passing through any of the 22 or 23

states which still had laws against miscegenation. If we did pass through them and we wanted to stop at a motel for accommodation for the night, would the manager be forced to deny us accommodation because we were racially mixed and were travelling with our "half-caste son Jamal"?

At every motel when we stopped for the night this question was hanging over us. In fact, nothing happened all the way across from Chicago to Los Angeles. We were accommodated in hotels without question or hostility, but there was the sheer uncertainty at every stop of waiting for the embarrassment, of clenching a fist nervously as I approached the reception to ask for a room for the night.

Because the nation had permitted laws against racially mixed marriages to continue until the early 1960s, every racially mixed couple in the country carried the cross of uncertainty as they travelled.

In the 1970s we were in the United States again. In this case it was clear that anti-miscegenation laws had begun to disappear in the late 1960s in spite of the Supreme Court's nervousness about giving a direct ruling on them. Was there residual racism still awaiting the traveller as well as the settled local?

One relevant experience for us came when we were driving in 1973 from Stanford University to the University of Washington in Seattle. My wife is the driver in our family, and we had covered that day some 300 or 400 miles. The children in the back were getting cranky and also Molly was tired. We decided to stop at the next motel if possible and spend the night there. The motel sign lit up said clearly "vacancy". We stopped and asked for accommodation for our family. The management regretted that they did not really have anything suitable. I argued that the sign clearly stated vacancy outside. The manager said that there was only one tiny room not well furnished, and certainly not large enough for the family. We asked to see it. It was small and dilapidated and presumably not usually used as a room for hotel guests. Since the rest of the family was so tired, I decided that we should take the room and just make the most of an uncomfortable night. A few minutes later I noticed from the window that the sign of the hotel still said "vacancy". Just then a car drove in. I thought that the people in the car were going to be told that the sign was a mistake; and that it should have been turned off. But it was soon clear that these latest white guests were being allocated a room. That cold sense of anger, that nervous twitch when one feels slighted and humiliated, had shattered whatever sense of ease I might have had. I pointed out the discrepancy to Molly, perhaps too loudly. By the time I had got dressed again in order to go out and confront the management, they were expecting me. They clearly knew their licence was at stake in the America of the 1970s if they coolly and blatantly practised racial discrimination. So they had a story. Someone had just cancelled a previous reservation. That was why they had not turned the light out saying "vacancy"; that is why they had the room, presumably large and comfortable, to offer the new white arrivals. I demanded to know why they had not given us first option, since they knew there were four of us crowded in a room not usually intended even for one guest. They were most apologetic. They would do their best to improve our room, bring in a television, add additional pillows; in short, become more hospitable now that the injustice towards a racially mixed family was discovered.

What we have in these two anecdotes was no direct racial victimization but the most subtle and insidious sense of uncertainty when a society has a tradition of racism and discrimination. Families like mine seemed condemned to periodic incidents that occasionally were blatant, more often subtle.

But the most exasperating humiliation of all is when one is not sure whether one is being racially humiliated. When my wife goes to a bank in Michigan to cash a cheque and is not asked for identification whereas I am always asked to prove my identity, can I be sure that the difference in treatment is racial, or merely the difference between a bank clerk she dealt with yesterday and a different clerk the next day who asked me for evidence of identification?

When I pass through the gates at Heathrow Airport with a lot of white people saying "nothing to declare" and none of the white people are stopped, but I am, can I be sure mine is simply the luck of the draw on this particular day, or was the customs man influenced in his choice of which cases to search by the fact that I was not white? I am prepared to concede that very often in such situations race is not a relevant factor. My wife's experiences with bank clerks who trust her may have been because her checks were usually for small amounts, while my own experiences with clerks who were more cautious might have been influenced by the slightly larger amounts I was seeking to withdraw.

My experiences at European airports when I am searched have probably nothing whatever to do with the fact that I am black. The balance of probability might well have been 99 per cent non-racial. But I bitterly resent having to wonder whether the 1 per cent chance of racial prejudice was in fact there. It is not necessarily the fault of the customs officers; it is the product of the history of my people.

I have often wondered whether a Jew, when singled out by customs officers at Heathrow Airport for a search, ever suffers the same nagging doubt about why he has been chosen. If a Jew does not, it is one more illustration of the basic paradox we are addressing ourselves to in this lecture, that Africans are not necessarily the most brutalized of peoples, but they are almost certainly the most humiliated in modern history. My own modest moments of doubt about my dignity as a human being have deep historical roots, going back to the slave trade and beyond. The blacks remain the worst victims of contempt; though not necessarily the worst casualties of brutality.

In this case we use brutalization to refer to a massive *physical* victimization. I am not of course saying that Africans have not been physically victimized, but have only been socially and psychologically humiliated. What I am saying is that in terms of sheer physical suffering there are other candidates for the title of ultimate martyrdom. For example, the Jews under the Nazi holocaust constitute one collective candidate for such brutal martyrdom. Six million of them perished in one of the coolest, most premeditated and most scientific exercises in genocide ever. Africans had been hunted once in order to be sold into slavery. The slave trade dehumanized its victims but it did not devalue them. On the contrary, a commercial price was put on each victim. The men and women lost their human dignity but they acquired a market value.

The Jews, on the other hand, were hunted down by the Nazis in order to be murdered. In that sense they were not only dehumanized; they were also totally devalued.

The blacks who were captured for the slave market were intended for future production on the plantations; the Jews who were captured for the concentration camps were often intended for speedy destruction in the gas chambers. The blacks exported to the Americas were designed to help to build a new civilization; the Jews destroyed under the Nazis were condemned as imperfections of the old civilization. Men, women and children died in those ghastly monuments of European racism at its most brutal. And blacks were not the victims of that ultimate excess in racism.

In North America earlier in modern history it is also arguable that the Indians, or native Americans, fell victim to greater brutality than did the imported blacks. On the whole Indians were widely regarded as pests for elimination, a danger to the success and prosperity of the immigrant civilization. The Indians were therefore fair game for war and for the human hunt. If the Nazis were guilty of a centralized form of genocide, white immigrants into North America were often guilty of decentralized genocide. Hundreds of thousands of Indians died as the wilderness was being conquered by the white immigrants. On the other hand, the whites regarded the blacks they had imported as a valuable source of labour. Blacks were not pests to be eliminated; they were cheap workers to be exploited. Both the Indians and the blacks were dehumanized, but only the Indians were devalued.

Genocidal also was the treatment of the aborigines in Australia. This again was partly a case of decentralized genocide, and partly the accident of new diseases which came with the white man and to which the local aboriginal populations capitulated. Perhaps the most deliberate of the genocidal exercises of Australia was the elimination of the native inhabitants of Tasmania. The white man succeeded in making that elimination virtually total.

Asia also has its contenders for the distinction of being particularly brutalized. The colonial and imperial wars which France and the United States waged in Indo-China after the Second World War have no real equivalent in Africa's experience. The casualties of war across the decades in Indo-China mounted into millions.

Nor must we forget the martyrdom of Hiroshima and Nagasaki as the first victims of nuclearized brutality. No one else so far can claim that horrifyingly dubious distinction.

In short, suffering defined in terms of physical victimization is not unique to the black experience, and has indeed found its worst manifestation outside the black world.

But brutality is one thing; humiliation is another. Humiliation takes the form of social and psychological degradation. It can sometimes take the form of being equated with goods and chattels; retaining value, indeed, but like the value of pigs on a farm, or cattle on a ranch.

Humiliation can also take the form of being systematically segregated, kept at a distance, identified as a source of potential social pollution. The caste system in places like India and systems of racial segregation like that of South Africa or of the old Southern states of America, are cases of institutionalized humiliation of the "lower" caste or "lower" race. This caste or race is culturally undervalued, socially segregated and psychologically demeaned.

It is in this sense that Africans and people of African ancestry might be regarded as having been the most humiliated in modern history.

Particularly important in this regard have been three inter-related systems of humiliation: the slave trade, European colonization of Africa, and continuing racial discrimination wherever black people live with white people.

The seventeenth century marked the beginning of the great escalation of the transatlantic slave trade. By the end of the sixteenth century little more than half a million black slaves from West Africa are estimated to have landed at destinations overseas. But in the following century that number was multiplied six times. In the course of the eighteenth century the number peaked to over six million Africans exported. By that time Britain's ships were carrying nearly half the slaves taken to America.[1]

Britain's share of the slave trade was partly a reflection of Britain's ascendancy in maritime and commercial activities among European states. That share of the slave trade was also connected with British access to the markets of the new world, especially North American and Caribbean. Thirdly, Britain gained an advantage in the slave trade because the parts of West Africa which Britain controlled (especially the coast

---

[1] For a brief statement on the subject consult Ronald Oliver and J. D. Fage, *A Short History of Africa* (Harmondsworth, Middlesex: Penguin Books), 1975 edn, p. 122.

between the Gold Coast and the Niger Delta) were the most thickly populated and economically best developed. These areas yielded more able-bodied Africans for the nefarious market of humans across the seas.

In terms of humiliation, the question does arise why it was Africa that was raided for slaves instead of other parts of the world. For example, in the Americas, why did not the white man use more systematically the local vanquished Indian populations as slave labour instead of importing blacks from thousands of miles away? In reality, there were efforts to use Indians as slave labour, especially in Spanish America. But those efforts where largely unsuccessful. The Indians just did not make good slave material for a variety of reasons. First, many Indian societies were still societies of hunters, whereas the West Africans who arrived came from traditions of settled cultivation. The latter life-style lent itself more neatly to plantation labour.

Secondly, nearness to the white man's diseases turned out to be more dangerous for Indians than for blacks. The blacks had better protective mechanisms in their own physiological constitutions and survived better in proximity to white families than did Indians.

Thirdly, Indians were being captured in their own home territory, in relatively familiar terrain. It was easier to run away from plantations and other centres of white masters. It was therefore more costly to devise systems of security to ensure that slaves did not run away. Imported Africans, on the other hand, were thousands of miles from their homes across many days of ocean travel. Escape from bondage into the wilderness was much harder for these Africans than for Indians.

Nevertheless, the white man's colonization of the Americas was accompanied by a savage lack of consideration for the Amerindian civilizations of those areas. The harsh treatment of the Indians did include, in some parts of the Americas, forcing them precisely into those forms of work for which they seemed to have little aptitude.

But then some Christian missionaries began to put up a determined defence of Indian interests. And the distinction between brutalization of Indians and humiliation of blacks began to emerge. There is the famous case of Las Casas who appealed to the Spanish sovereigns, Ferdinand and Isabella, asking them to intervene and obtain justice for the Indians. A debate raged between those who regarded Indians as an inferior race that must learn to serve the white man and those who, like Las Casas, were pained by the suffering of the conquered race.

In the end, something approaching a compromise seems to have been reached. Las Casas so pitied the Indians that he encouraged importation of Africans into Spanish America. The argument was partly Aristotelian: that since the Indians died so easily in slave labour, the Almighty did not intend them to be slaves. Since blacks did not die, they must be natural slaves. So the syllogism went. The humiliation of blacks was given both Aristotelian and biblical vindication.

But why did not the Europeans raid North Africa for Arab and Berber slaves? Why did they not go all the way to India and import Indian slaves? Why pick on Africans as material for enslavement?

One reason was simply geographical. The slaves were needed for the Caribbean or North or South America and West Africa was much nearer than the Indian subcontinent. South Asians were later virtually induced into labour as indentured workers, but never as outright chattel slaves as Africans were.

Another reason why Europeans regarded Africans as more legitimate material for enslavement was the cultural distance between European and African civilizations. The Africans seemed to the Europeans so "primitive" that they were deemed fitted for menial roles, including the role of slaves.

Thirdly there was the racial distance between the white slavers and the black slaves. The very terminology that Europeans used to refer to their complexion as white and to that of Africans as black emphasized the extremities of the spectrum of pigmentation, the polar opposites of colour and race. It was easier for the Europeans, therefore, to dehumanize those that were furthest from them in culture and complexion, and proceed to enslave them.

The fourth reason why Africans were regarded as fair game was simply their military weakness. Their combat culture of spears and bows and arrows was no match for the new firearms. On the contrary, sometimes Europeans traded firearms for slaves, rewarding one set of Africans with guns so that they might continue to procure other sets of Africans for the slave market.

But towards the end of the eighteenth century and the beginning of the nineteenth things began to change. Britain, once the leading slave-trading nation, became the leading abolitionist. British ships sailed the high seas to control or thwart smuggling in slaves.

This is one of the peculiarities of western capitalism in its historical interaction with Africa. In the earlier phases of the development of that capitalism, slavery was an asset and needed to be cultivated and promoted. But in the late eighteenth and certainly in the course of the nineteenth century, capitalism, far from being enthusiastic about slavery and the slave trade, was becoming hostile to it. The leading abolitionists were indeed the leading capitalist powers. Britain was indeed such a power at the time. And in the United States the North was more developed in capitalist terms than the southern states. It was the North which was abolitionist and the South which was in defence of the slave system.

Why was mature capitalism more hostile to slavery and ready to save Africa from its continuation?

The reasons are varied. They include the fact that technology and the more mature capitalism had reached a stage where slave labour was less efficient than wage labour. A slave was often bought for life, whereas a wage worker was often hired for a week. An ailing worker could be fired and replaced at next to no cost, but the worst time to sell a slave is when he is ailing.

Owning slaves included some responsibility for non-productive members of the slave's family, including little children and very old people. But workers could be hired at a minimum salary with little consideration of whether that was enough to keep the worker's children and elderly folk alive.

Yet another reason why capitalism by that time was leaning towards wage labour and against slave labour was simply the pace of urbanization in the metropolitan countries themselves and the large pool of cheap labour which was created as a result. One did not have to brave the seas or the diseases of West Africa to get cheap labour. It was available not far from Manchester or Philadelphia.

But while Britan was becoming the leading abolitionist nation in history, it was simultaneously building the biggest empire in history. British capitalism was indeed by the nineteenth century hostile to slavery, but it was at the same time becoming much more favourable to imperialism. In Africa, the British flag was flying before long from the Niger Delta in the West to the source of the Nile in East Africa, and from Cairo in the north to the Cape of Good Hope in the south. Another form of humiliation was under way. It is true that colonization as a form of humiliation was far from being unique to Africa, but at any rate colonization was as complete in the African continent as almost anywhere else in the world.

In 1884 Bismarck called the Congress of Berlin. Fifteen western countries meditated over the rules for the partition of Africa. The scramble for the continent was on, and sometimes carried the danger of engulfing the European rivals vying for new possessions in Africa. The conference in Berlin was designed to be a pre-emptive measure to reduce the threats of inter-European conflicts as the powers went around carving portions of the continent for themselves.

Much later an English writer, George Orwell, converted the year 1984 virtually into a symbol of doom, a horrifying model of negative Utopia. But for much of Africa it was 1884, rather than 1984, which was the symbol of doom. The Berlin Congress opened in 1884 to help seal the fate of the continent for at least another century. The nightmare of European penetration and colonization of Africa was now truly under way.

European ambitions were of course varied. There was interest in new sources of raw materials; new potential markets for European goods once a demand was cultivated and a purchasing power created; new outlets for European surplus population regardless of the crisis of habitability in parts of Africa; new outlets for European capital to be invested in risky but excitingly challenging ventures in Africa; new potential sources of energy with all those waterfalls and subsequently with all that coal, uranium and oil; new souls to convert to Christianity — in short, new worlds to conquer.

The European colonizers included France with its share of western and equatorial Africa; Belgium controlling Zaïre and later Rwanda and Burundi; Portugal with its empire in Angola, Mozambique and Guinea-Bissau; Italy which subsequently controlled not only Libya but also Somalia and briefly Ethiopia; Spain with its tiny empire in western Sahara; and Germany until the First World War with an African empire which included what is now mainland Tanzania, Cameroun, Togo and Namibia.

But by far the largest empire was Britain's. Nigeria alone contained more people than the whole of French Africa added together. And until 1910 Britain also effectively ruled South Africa, destined even then to be the richest and more technologically developed of African countries.

But South Africa brings us to the third paradigm of humiliation after the slave trade and colonization: that of institutionalized racism and racial segregation. In many ways the South African phenomenon is the worst insult of them all. After all, the slave trade was a hit-and-run exercise as the slavers captured people and quickly abducted them and exported them abroad. Colonization was something that happened to many other parts of the world in the wake of European technological and military preeminence. But the worst insult to Africa is to have within its own ancestral continent the last bastion of institutionalized African humiliation remaining in the modern world.

Here again it may be instructive to start with a personal anecdote. Some years ago, when I was still teaching at Makerere University in Uganda, I received an invitation to go and give some lectures at the University of Cape Town in South Africa. I was then and continue to be today in favour efforts made by African states to isolate South Africa diplomatically. I shall explain my position on the policy of boycotting South Africa more fully later on, but let me simply say here that I am less sure about isolating South Africa intellectually in terms of preventing the free flow of ideas and knowledge into the Republic. The question which arose then was whether my visit to South Africa was to be regarded as a violation of the diplomatic boycott of South Africa or simply as a contribution to the intellectual enlightenment of the racist society. Before making up my mind for certain which way to go, I knew what my minimum conditions were going to be. These were, first, that I should be able to address racially mixed audiences if I did go; secondly that I should be free to say whatever I wanted; thirdly, that I should be free to take my wife with me on the visit. I chose the last condition in order to test the South African system at its most sensitive. I communicated these conditions to the University of Cape Town. The reply from the university indicated that they could guarantee the fulfilment of my first condition, that of being able to address racially mixed audiences. They were also prepared to gamble on my second condition, that I should be free to say whatever I wanted. But the condition which seemed impossible to meet was precisely the one which, in most civilized societies, would be regarded as a matter of course, that is, that I would be able to take my wife with me, at our own expense, if she were free to join me on the trip. My prospective hosts at the University of Cape Town had consulted their lawyers, and they were told categorically that it was out of the question for me to go with my English wife to South Africa without risking proceedings against me under the Republic's Immorality Laws and laws against "miscegenation".

Some years later, I related this incident in a lecture to a joint meeting of the Royal Commonwealth Society and the Royal African Society in London. My topic was on academic freedom in Africa. I argued that there were occasions when academic freedom in a particular society suffered because other freedoms did not exist. The freedom to mate across a racial line was at first glance unrelated to academic life. And yet the academic freedom of the University of Cape Town was compromised because the society as a whole had laws against mixed mating and mixed marriages.

My lecture was published in the journals of the two organizations that I had addressed at the joint meeting. I received a letter from the Office of the Prime Minister of South Africa. He had instructed his secretary to let me know that I had been misinformed by the University of Cape Town. The Prime Minister asserted that the laws in question did not apply to me. Subsequently, the Vice-Chancellor of the University of Cape Town was publicly reprimanded for misinforming foreign scholars. In reality, the apparent attempt by the Prime Minister, Mr Vorster, to assure me that the laws against mixed mating did not apply to me was presumably part of the strategy at the time to facilitate greater interaction between South Africans and Africans from elsewhere in the continent.

The letter from the Prime Minister's office could be interpreted as an invitation to me to go ahead and apply for a visa for both Molly and myself. But my own reservations about visiting a country where some mixed marriages were exempt from the laws and others were not was still strong. In any case, the whole experience took me back to the time when President Idi Amin in Uganda wanted to send me and a few others to South Africa. Amin said he had chosen us carefully, partly with the view to demonstrating to the racists in South Africa that Africans could think. I did not want to be used in this way as a thinking specimen, nor was I convinced that dialogue as expounded by the South African government was either sincere or meaningful. I suggested to Field-Marshal Amin a method of testing Prime Minister Vorster's sincerity. Previously, some of our people had studied in South Africa. My boss at Makerere at one time, Principal Y. K. Lule, had studied in South Africa in his younger days. (Lule was later to be the first president to succeed Idi Amin after his fall.) Lule's boss when I was at Makerere, Minister of Education Luyimbazi-Zake, had also studied in South Africa. Did Vorster's concept of "dialogue" include a reversing of the flow of education, so that young South Africans could study in black universities elsewhere in Africa without being harassed by South African authorities or treated as refugees? Would Vorster permit free interaction among African youth across his own borders? In the words I used in a letter to Idi Amin in October 1971:

> the question is not simply whether Africans are prepared to go to South Africa, but also whether the Government of South Africa is prepared to facilitate travel by young South Africans to black African countries. . . . Your Excellency, what I am suggesting is that we should carry the debate on the issue of dialogue downwards from the pinnacle of relations between Heads of Governments to the more modest interaction between university students and young people. Further, we should firmly put the ball in South Africa's court by challenging their sincerity in this way.

When I made the proposal I had got Idi Amin at the right moment. He said that before the end of the week I would hear something. I did hear something; he offered ten scholarships to young South Africans to study at Makerere, and added five scholarships for Namibians.

My faith in young people as a potential vanguard of the struggle for a new order in Africa was later vindicated both in South Africa after Soweto and in Amin's Uganda when many young people joined the liberating forces on their way to Kampala. In 1971 I was simply trying to persuade Amin to facilitate the process of contact between the young of Africa, instead of staging ceremonial summit meetings with the likes of John Vorster.

I think I can say that I played a part, fully documented, in pulling Amin back from collaboration with South African racists. Few aspects of Amin's policies and views lasted as long as his conversion to militant opposition to apartheid. It is now many years since that day when, in a packed assembly hall at Makerere University, President Amin publicly handed over to me a cable he had just received from the Prime Minister of South Africa. The audience in the assembly hall (the Main Hall at Makerere) did not know what the cable was about, but Amin had decided to consult me on the South African issue and was making a public display of it. But the advice he got from me in confidence helped to draw him back from his initial flirtation with the racists of southern Africa. Grand dialogue between white South Africa and black Africa outside did not make much sense before an adequate dialogue had begun to take place between white South Africans and black South Africans within their own country. The worst insult to Africa continues to be the distance which has been created between these two groups by the elaborate system of racial discrimination and segregation in that doomed society.

Part of the problem relates to the wider world of capitalism. We mentioned earlier that western industrial capitalism had by the nineteenth century become hostile to slavery, but at the same time it had become congenial to imperialism and colonization. Britain led the way in freeing the black slaves; but Britain also led the way in colonizing black countries in Africa.

The system in South Africa is an amalgam of slavery and colonization. Apartheid shares with slavery the assumptions of hereditary caste roles, that is, status based partly on descent and partly on ascriptive rules of master and servant. Just as racism and contempt for black people was at the core of the slave trade, so once again are racism and contempt for black people at the core of apartheid.

But South Africa is not only a case of colonization of Africa by non-Africans, but is also a case of reflecting the wider world of western economic imperialism.

We might therefore infer that apartheid as slavery is something which the western powers would genuinely abhor, just as they abhorred the transatlantic slave trade in the nineteeenth century. But apartheid as imperialism is something which western powers identify with, just as they identified with empire-building in the nineteenth century.

This dialectic was feasible and even successful in the nineteenth century. Britain could at once be the leading abolitionist power and the leading empire-builder. The question which arises today is whether Britain can effectively work for the end of apartheid as a racial system without losing the economic benefits of white-dominated South Africa as an imperial system.

What are the western powers to do in the face of this dilemma? They once managed to have their abolitionist cake and eat it too. Can they now continue to eat the fruit of white-dominated South Africa and at the same time disgorge the accompanying poison of apartheid?

So far there have been two dominant views of the role of western investment in South Africa. One view has been to the effect that western investment helps to liberalize the regime and may help to avert violence as a solution.

The second view is that Western investment consolidates the power of the racist regime and makes effective social transformation more difficult to attain. Let us take each of these views in turn.

The view that western investment is liberalizing partly rests on the West's own historical precedents. Industrialization in England gradually resulted in greater internal democratization. There was a growth of the urban proletariat, a struggle for the rights of collective bargaining, an expansion of the franchise first to the middle classes and then to the working classes, the emergence of new political parties, and the institutionalization of the open society in the wake of the Industrial Revolution. If western investment in South Africa has the same industrializing impact, should we not also expect it to have the same democratizing effect?

A related line of reasoning is that the western presence in South Africa, and the consciousness of the western model, could stimulate South African society by example; this is the demonstration effect. Raising wages in western firms within the purview of South African society would gradually help to change the standards of that society upwards. In the United States the Sullivan Principles for South Africa are intended to guide American investors morally and help them reconcile the pursuit of profit with the maintenance of minimum standards of economic equity.

Another aspect of the school of thought which regards western investment as a liberalizing force in South Africa is the belief that western influence on the government in Pretoria can only be as great as the West's economic importance to Pretoria. A dismantling of western economic empires and investment structures in South Africa would severely undermine any liberalizing leverage that the West might have over the regime in power.

The opposing school of thought views western investment as having the effect of consolidating the racist regime. With that investment apartheid gets the *de facto* support of the immense economic power of international capitalism at large, and this in turn helps to give greater legitimacy to the racial system as a whole within the Republic.

Because of western investment influential western nations acquire a vested interest in the survival of the present regime. Some even believe in their heart of hearts that apartheid with stability is better than black majority rule at the risk of chaos.

Thirdly, western investment, to the extent to which it increases South Africa's prosperity, enhances the vested interest of local whites in the system as it now stands, and discourages pressure for meaningful and liberalizing reform.

Fourthly, western investment increases the regime's capacity to co-opt a minority of Africans into relatively privileged positions and distribute enough benefits to the wider population to delay a radicalization of political consciousness among the masses of the oppressed.

Fifthly, western investment, by needing stability, helps to encourage the regime to maintain its structure of repression as a method of assuring stability.

Steve Biko was a martyr to a brutal infrastructure of stability — and western investment contributed towards it.

My own position on the matter is a dialectical combination of the two. I accept the proposition that western investment has helped to consolidate the regime, but I also accept the expectation that western investment may indeed liberalize the system. Yet I go on to say that the two processes together will in time create a revolutionary situation in South Africa. On the whole, revolutions in history have tended to occur not when the people are at their lowest and their most indigent, but precisely when matters are beginning to improve. Revolutionary situations in the normal course of historical change often occur when progress is being made but not fast enough to overtake expectations, nor radical enough to close the gap of relative deprivation.

This theory is partly neo-Marxist though I am not myself a Marxist of any kind. The proposition here is that making South Africa's economic system more modern helps to increase its incompatibility with racism, and therefore helps to dig the grave of apartheid itself. The economic substructure in South Africa's society is thus able to change more rapidly than the racial superstructure: and just as capitalism developed earlier to such a level that it could no longer tolerate slavery, so capitalism in South Africa is bound to develop quite shortly to a level when it can no longer tolerate institutionalized segregation.

Capitalism in South Africa will produce its own grave-diggers, especially a black proletarian class. Initially it was a case of blacks taking over jobs which whites would not touch. But more and more the system may have to expand black labour in areas of potential competition with whites.

Black economic consciousness is already on the increase, as industrial action erupts from time to time to demand adjustment in the system of rewards. Black political consciousness has known its moments of militant assertiveness already, ranging from the martyrdom of Sharpeville to the heroism of Soweto.

Then there will be border capitalism near the Bantustans or newly created homelands, providing additional potential pockets of resistance and change.

What I am saying is that western investment still has a role to play in South Africa, the role of helping to create conditions for a revolutionary uprising before the end of this century. Creating those conditions does require a partial liberalization of the system. Opponents of the regime need more opportunities to meet and discuss strategies; movements need freedom of manoeuvre: militants need some breathing space for organization; grievances need freedom of articulation; the races need opportunities for mutual communication.

Western investment can help create the first genuine black proletarian class in Africa, the workers of the Republic of

South Africa, whether or not they are legally citizens or stateless.

But for the West to exert its leverage on the regime effectively towards liberalization, it is important that the divestment movement in the West should in turn exert pressure in the metropole. No western government and certainly no western investors will feel the urge to ask the South African regime to liberalize, unless the demands in western Europe and North America are pitched at a higher level of rupture. By asking western governments and investors to divest from South Africa, we may simply succeed in making the investors improve the working conditions of their own workers in South Africa and in making western governments plead for democratic concessions from the South African regime.

By demanding a total western withdrawal, we may help the liberalizing tendency to get under way. By enabling liberalization to proceed, we may help the revolutionaries with their final confrontation.

But western leverage also gains if there is a tiny bit of collective western withdrawal, just enough to worry the regime in South Africa about the increasing menace of global isolation. For example, I have no doubt in my mind that universities in the western world have the moral obligation to take the lead in divestment. Universities are great centres not only of learning but also of liberal enlightenment in the West. By withdrawing their investments from firms with extensive dealings with South Africa, they will be contributing towards increasing western leverage. While total western withdrawal would by definition drastically reduce any influence the West might have on the South African regime, selective and well planned western withdrawal could *increase* western influence as the regime struggles to make more concessions in order to avert further withdrawal.

Let me now summarize the argument. By increasing the prosperity of South Africa, western investment is contributing to the growth of the first really large and significant black proletarian class in Africa. By the demonstration effect of western investors' own firms and wages, they raise the expectations of workers elsewhere in South Africa, and contribute towards the growth of militant economic consciousness. By putting pressure on the South African regime to make liberal concessions and increase the liberties of its citizens, western governments and investors help the opponents of the regime in South Africa to know each other and organize better for additional pressures in the future. But ultimately the white-dominated regime will not give up power simply through the liberalizing process. They will never reach a stage when they would peacefully accept, for example, the principle of "one man, one vote" in choosing the rulers of the country.

It follows, therefore, that the ultimate solution is a violent revolution in South Africa. And my own conviction is that conditions of violent revolution in a racially segregated society can best be created in conditions where new economic classes drawn from the oppressed are demanding new rewards, and there is sufficient freedom in the society to enable revolution-aries to recruit and organize for the final confrontation with the system of injustice.

Mind you, when the revolution does come, western investors will get no credit for it, nor will they deserve any credit. After all, their motives for investing have never been concerned with creating conditions for fundamental change. The investors were digging the grave of apartheid by default, by the iron law of unintended consequences.

But the West as a whole could improve its chances in the post-revolutionary South Africa by supporting liberation fighters there sooner than it supported liberation fighters in Zimbabwe or Namibia. It is not true that the West is faced with a clear alternative, either to continue investing in South Africa or to support liberation movements aiming for change. The West could do both. By investing in the economic system it would, as I indicated, be helping the earlier phases of the revolution to come. But the West must also be ready to give moral support to the guerrilla struggle when it gets under way, and permit the movements to raise funds freely in western capitals. It would be difficult for western governments to provide arms and ammunition to liberation fighters directly, but they could at least shut a blind eye to movements of arms destined for the liberation fighters. This would be the other side of the coin of an arms embargo on the Pretoria regime itself, which the United Nations imposed in 1977.

The twin strategies for the West for the future, therefore, are, firstly, continuing but selective investment in South Africa, and secondly, moral and material support for the liberation fighters in the great test of will in the years ahead.

South Africa might well turn out to be the theatre of the last great battle against Africa's historic cross of humiliation. The concept of race will not vanish after South Africa is liberated. Race as a concept of biological differentiation is a permanent fact of life; but racism as a concept of social graduation is a finite historical phenomenon whose end may be in sight, though not necessarily in our own lifetime. In a few decades in the twentieth century the human race has reached remarkable consensus about the moral illegitimacy of racism. Votes against apartheid in the United Nations are almost unanimous these days, though there used to be genuinely split votes less than two decades ago. The phenomenon of injustice and racial prejudice is quite old, but the phenomenon of sustained segregation of races is a child of recent history. Both forms of racism are transitory and finite. They may be very present in our daily lives today not only in Africa, but also in England and of course in the United States and elsewhere. But on balance Africa's cross of humiliation may well be put to eternal rest in the twenty-first century. The slave trade has ended except for a trickle in disguise. Direct political colonization is in its last chapter. And institutionalized racism is under a clear, emphatic and almost universally acclaimed sentence of death.

Now, why am I convinced that racism is on the way out? Why am I so confident that the twentieth century might well be the last century with any significant racial problems on the globe?

In order to answer that, let me distinguish between two forms of human solidarity. One kind of solidarity is based on a biological relationship among the members of the group. The relationship may amount to an extended family, or a clan, or a tribe — or indeed a race. The biological relationship could be real, in the sense that the group is descended from some joint ancestors, or it could be presumed by the members of the group.

The second kind of solidarity is based on an economic relationship, again real or presumed. The clearest case of this kind of solidarity comes out of class consciousness. The workers who feel united because they see themselves in a shared economic predicament, or employers who are drawn together out of a sense of shared economic survival, are part of the phenomenon of economic solidarity.

The history of the world so far seems to indicate a decline in the power of biological solidarity, and a rise in the influence of economic forms of unity. Thus, such biological foundations of unity as the broad extended family, as the clan and the tribe, have certainly either declined drastically in the northern hemisphere of the world or are strongly on the defensive. In the United Kingdom only parts of Scotland and Ireland seem to retain a strong sense of clan solidarity.

Tribalism, in the sense of a larger group that sees itself as having been descended from a particular tribal ancestor, has almost disappeared in the western world as a whole.

The question arises whether the fate of these other forms of biological solidarity — the extended family, the clan and the tribe — will also befall racism and race consciousness as the last political bulwarks of the mythology of kith and kin.

My own conviction is that racism will go the way of tribalism, and gradually make its exit from human experience except on a very modest scale.

In Europe, tribalism was almost the first to go among these forms of biological alignments; racism may well be the last to go. In Africa, on the other hand, racism is likely to end first, following the liberartion of southern Africa. But tribalism may last much longer, though ultimately also doomed to extinction in the generation that will follow.

Europe has put its tribal house in order by ordering tribalism out. But racism has come in through the back door, especially in the wake of European imperialism and its decline. In Africa tribalism is part of the habitat for the time being: it is racism that is about to be forced out into historical oblivion.

The coming extinction of racism in human experience has been facilitated by the transformation of international diplomacy and international politics. Never before in history has the world community been as multiracial as it is today. The liberation of so many non-white countries in Asia, Africa and the Pacific, coupled with a system of communications which has transformed this planet into a single global diplomatic system, have together brought into being the largest multiracial society in history, mankind itself in the last quarter of the twentieth century.

Given then the multiracialism of world diplomacy at the present day, the rules of international conduct have never been more hostile to racism. Almost no diplomat today is likely to stand before the General Assembly of the United Nations and express views which are based on theories of racial superiority and racial inferiority. Many western diplomats in different parts of the world might themselves still be racist, but the rhetoric of world diplomacy would tend to force them to disguise their racism. Virtually all major votes against apartheid in the United Nations and its agencies are carried these days by overwhelming majorities, sometimes virtually unanimously. Yet only three or four decades ago there would have been a real and significant division of opinion among world diplomats discussing either apartheid in South Africa or racial incidents in the United States.

What is emerging is considerable consensus within the world system on issues of race, a consensus sometimes merely rhetorical, but nevertheless part of the reality of the contemporary world. In the future people will quarrel over incomes, jobs and commodities. They will quarrel less and less over race and tribe.

If solidarity based on economic interests is rising, while solidarity based on biological kinship is declining, what is the likely outcome for the future?

I personally believe that a classless society is impossible. There will always be gradations among human beings based on differences in either political power, economic advantage, or indeed both. Karl Marx's prediction that after the proletarian revolution a society heads for a classless arrangement is simply a lot of wishful thinking. Economic classes are here to stay. What we must do is to keep to a minimum the differences between them in power and advantage.

On the other hand, racism and tribalism are not here to stay. The ultimate destination for humankind is not a classless society, but a detribalized society, at least in the sense of the final elimination of all forms of political and economic allegiances based on the solidarity of kith and kin. Even the nuclear family will one day have to give up the special privileges of nepotism in most areas of social conduct.

One of mankind's last great battles against racism will be fought not in southern Africa but in the streets of Birmingham, the ghettos of Detroit, the harbours of Marseilles, and the motels of the rest of the western world. In other words, the West will be one of the last grand arenas of the human struggle against the more subtle forms of racial injustice.

One of the last great battlegrounds of mankind against tribalism will be fought in Africa, as blacks learn to live with other blacks without extensive structures of ethnic nepotism and discrimination. As for class struggle, it can have no final battlefield. When southern Africans emerge with all the scars of racial warfare, when the rest of black Africa emerges eager at least to do away with the invisible tribal tattoos of the body scars which mark off one ethnic group from another, when Europeans at last discover how to deal with non-white people as fellow passengers of Spaceship Earth, there will still be one residual and infinite moral engagement awaiting them all: class struggle in pursuit of even greater social justice.

But is class formation merely a product of economic forces? In an imperial system the role of culture in class formation is often underestimated. The culture of the imperial power, or of the governing race, acquires a level of prestige which often goes beyond its economic utility. In much of Africa men and women who were initiated into the verbal and literary skills of their masters rose to new heights of influence as a result, independently of their initial economic position in society. The commanding heights of each political system had two ladders leading up to them: the ladder of economic affluence and the ladder of cultural influence. It is to these complexities of culture contact and cultural stratification that we shall turn in the next lecture.

LECTURE 3

A Clash of Cultures

Not so long ago I had lunch with a French-speaking African friend of mine. As a child he was attacked by polio, and his limbs were beginning to give way. A debate started in his family as to whether he should be thrown into the river. He had come into the world seemingly in an imperfect condition, and the idea of throwing him into the river and letting him drown was in order to enable him to return in better condition as a subsequent child. A theory of reincarnation had been converted into a form of therapy for a child deformed by polio.

As the debate within the family was raging, my friend's condition fortunately began to improve. This improvement finally tilted the balance in favour of those who saw therapy in terms of offerings and prayer, rather than in the drastic "surgical" decision of throwing the baby into a river to drown.

My friend is now a learned scholar in both French and English. He shows almost no sign of his polio affliction apart from a partial stiffening of his right arm and hand. His personal history is part of the history of medical science in Africa. His family has learned a lot during his single lifetime.

Yet Africa is still in a state of transition. In the field of scientific explanation, Africans are having to change their minds about a lot of things. What causes rain? We are beginning to be converted to the proposition that droughts are not caused by a surplus of twin babies born in a particular year.

What causes disease? Whenever I have indigestion I still have a residual puzzlement whether it might not have been caused by the evil eye of either somebody hungry or somebody greedy who caught a glimpse of my jaws chewing away. Yet I do find relief when I turn to Alka Seltzer.

Clearly Africa is not the nearest in culture to the western world, yet the continent has indeed been experiencing perhaps the fastest pace of westernization this century of anywhere in the non-western world. What are the causes of this paradox? What are the implications?

To understand the full ramifications it would be useful to relate the process of westernization in Africa to seven functions of culture in societies generally.

First, culture provides lenses of perception, a way of looking at reality, a world view. In what way has the western impact modified the African view of the world?

Secondly, culture provides standards of evaluation. What is good and what is evil, what is beautiful and what is ugly, what is legitimate and what is illegitimate are all rooted in criteria provided by culture. In what way has the western impact transformed or distorted Africa's standards of evaluation?

Thirdly, culture conditions motivation. What motivates individuals to act or to refrain from acting, what inspires individuals to perform well or to really exert themselves, is partly inspired by cultural factors.

Fourthly, culture is a medium of communication. The communicative aspects of culture range from language in the literal sense to physical gestures and modes of dress.

Fifthly, culture provides a basis of stratification, a pecking order in society. Status, rank and class are partly the outcome of a cultural order. Has the pecking order in Africa changed as a result of the western impact? Are new classes in the making in the continent in response to Africa's interaction with Europe in the cultural field?

Then there is the link between culture and the means of production, which is in part a link between culture and economics. Has westernization in Africa modified and transformed the means and modes of production? And what is the primary force in historical change in any case? Is it culture change or economic progress?

The seventh major function of culture in society is the

function of defining identity, of determining who are the "we" in a given situation and who are the "they". Have identities in Africa changed as a result of Africa's interaction with the western world?

Let us now examine these seven areas of cultural impact in greater detail, and estimate why cultures which are so different and so distant from western ways could at the same time have so rapidly capitulated to the western cultural challenge.

In assessing the relationship between culture and perception, it may be worth our while to remind ourselves of Thomas Kuhn's study, *The Structure of Scientific Revolutions*. Kuhn distinguishes between normal science, signifying the continuities of scientific thought, and scientific revolution, which comes when the whole view of looking at reality undergoes fundamental and relatively speedy change. Kuhn wrote an earlier book entitled *The Copernican Revolution* which to some extent anticipated some of the ideas of his later and more influential work concerning scientific revolutions generally. What Copernicus revolutionized was our way of looking at the universe. In a book published in 1543 Copernicus corrected Ptolemy's and Aristotle's versions of the universe, and thereby challenged the ethnocentrism of the human race itself. Humanity had until then regarded the world as the centre of the universe. Copernicus struck at this collective planetary ethnocentrism of mankind, and provided foundations for both moral humility and a scientific understanding of the planets. Copernicus thus effected a revolution in our perception of reality, a shift in what Thomas Kuhn would call a "paradigm". Charles Darwin a little nearer to our day was another scientific revolutionary in this sense. He has in fact been compared to Copernicus in terms of cutting man down to size. As one writer has put it:

> Just as the Copernican system of astronomy had deposed the Earth from its central place in the universe, so Darwinism seemed to dethrone man from his natural conclusion of the churchmen when Darwin published another book, *The Descent of Man*, in 1871. In this work he marshalled the evidence that man is related to all animal life.[1]

[1] L. S. Stravrianos, *Man's Past and Present: A Global History* (Englewood Cliffs, N.J.: Prentice-Hall, 1971), pp. 270-3.

Other scientific revolutions will of course include the discoveries of figures like Isaac Newton and Albert Einstein. All these were major shifts in scientific paradigms. They are also part of the history of the scientific civilization which the western world later came to transmit to African societies.

Although Thomas Kuhn's theory was intended almost entirely to deal with scientific revolutions, what we plan to raise here in this lecture is the issue of cultural revolutions in a sense much wider than that intended by Mao's China in the 1960s. Just as the Darwins and Newtons of this world cause a major paradigm shift in the methodology of science, other individuals and processes sometimes stimulate almost equally fundamental changes in culture. We are familiar with religious revolutions. The rise of Islam in Arabia in the seventh century was a major paradigm shift for the Arabs, away from polytheism and idolatry to a new and militant monotheism. The message of Jesus was also revolutionary in fundamental ways, though it was slower in establishing itself within its area than the message of the Prophet Muhammad had been in his own lifetime.

We also know that in economic thought there have been great stages in transformation. The legacies of David Ricardo and Adam Smith provided a liberal capitalist paradigm which lasted almost totally unmodified until the Keynesian revolution in English economic thought in the interwar years of this century. Keynesian economics has itself coexisted all along with an alternative paradigm, the Marxian and neo-Marxist school of political economy. Again, all these three economic traditions (legacies of Adam Smith, Karl Marx and John Maynard Keynes) have found their way into Africa and entered Africa's intellectual melting pot.

A variety of western paradigms (both scientific and cultural) converged on the African continent together. The question that arose was whether they in turn would occasion a broad cultural revolution in the African mind, for better or for worse.

In the history of science a revolutionary crisis occurs when there is a persistent anomaly in the traditional paradigm which cannot be explained, and which makes the paradigm unable to accommodate certain realities or solve certain puzzles. As Kuhn himself puts it:

In science . . . novelty emerges only with difficulty, manifested by resistance against a background provided by expectation. Initially, only the anticipated and usual are experienced even under circumstances where anomaly is later to be observed. Further acquaintance, however, does result in awareness of something wrong or does relate the effect to something that has gone wrong before. The awareness of anomaly opens a period in which conceptual categories are adjusted until the initially anomalous has become the anticipated. At this point the discovery has been completed.[2]

In a cultural revolution the fundamental change may indeed occur when existing cultural visions are inadequate for the new realities. This was certainly so with regard to the rise of Islam in Arabia.

But although Islam was indeed stimulated by non-Arab ideas from Judaism and Christianity, it was on the whole an indigenous eruption among the Arabs. The cultural revolution in the Africa of the twentieth century is not just stimulated by the West, it is basically a case of African cultures gradually capitulating to the aggressive conquering force of western civilization.

The power of western paradigms in Africa was increased because of a basic alliance between western science and western Christianity as transmitted in missionary schools in Africa. Religion is one way of explaining reality; science is another way, though they are not necessarily incompatible. The carriers of Christianity into Africa were also the carriers of western secular education. The missionaries built schools not simply to teach the catechism and the Bible, but also to teach mathematics, biology and one or more European language.

Much more so than in colonial India or occupied Egypt, the colonial powers in Africa south of the Sahara gave the missionaries virtually a free rein outside strongly Islamic areas. So, whereas colonized Indians and colonized Egyptians had to

---

[2] Thomas S. Kuhn, *The Structure of Scientific Revolutions* (Chicago and London: University of Chicago Press), 1967 edn, p. 64. For the application of Kuhn's ideas on theories of development consult Aidan Foster-Carter, "From Rostow to Gunder Frank: Conflicting Paradigms in the Analysis of Underdevelopment", *Word Development* (March 1976), Vol. 4, No. 2, pp. 167-80.

contend mainly with western secular and scientific paradigms, colonized black Africans had to contend with both these secular paradigms and a highly institutionalized Christian missionary effort at the same time.

I am not saying there were no missionary institutions in India and other parts of Asia, or in the Muslim world. I am simply saying that in countries which had what Westerners regarded as a high religious culture (like Hinduism, Buddhism and Islam), the Christian effort was careful and circumspect, fearing a backlash from militant religious "zealots". But black Africans were not regarded as having a "high religious culture", but as having at best "folk" or "tribal" religions. The missionaries could challenge these with impunity, and the imperial power let them do it, confident that there would be no significant backlash from "tribal" zealots.

This combined western onslaught on the African mind, linking the sacred with the secular, allying science with religion, created a particularly strong cultural revolution in Africa, not least because traditional African cultures themselves did not differentiate between secular knowledge and sacred wisdom.

I have already referred to the antiquated medical paradigms within which many African societies once tried to treat their sick. As a child I watched one of my closest friends shiver and groan his way to death. I now suspect that the lad had pneumonia, but his mother was sure that the boy's condition had something to do with the curse of the owl. In Swahili we sometimes refer to the owl as *babae watoto*, the father of children. Westerners used to regard the owl as wise. So did we in East Africa. But in addition we invested the owl with powers reminiscent of the Pied Piper of Hamelin, the power to produce the kind of noises that could summon a child away to his death.

My friend's mother in Mombasa displayed special signs and offerings at the entrance of the house, desperately trying to break the spell of the owl. But the child moaned his way to death, himself converted to the proposition that he was under the captivating curse of *babae watoto*. I wept bitterly on behalf of my playmate when he died. I cursed the owl in return.

Even if we had known my Mombasa friend was suffering from pneumonia, that particular child might have died. But what about my French-speaking friend of later years who was nearly thrown into a river to drown as therapy for polio? Clearly the medical paradigm which had threatened his life did deserve to change under the impact of the West.

Less clear as candidates for change were the religious paradigms. Can we be really sure, unless we are believers, which religion is superior to which?

The gods of many indigenous religions were gods of justice, ready to inflict pain if necessary. The God of Christianity was a god of love who nevertheless approved of suffering as a way to God.

The gods of African traditional religions were often gods of bravery. The God of Christianity urged you to "turn the other cheek". The gods of Africa rewarded the warriors; the God of Christianity canonized the martyrs. The gods of Africa made certain trees sacred, certain mountains holy, certain animals brothers and sisters. The God of Christianity talked of man alone as being made in the image of God. The other inhabitants of the planet lacked that level of sacredness, and were only there to serve man.

In the end the feminine virtues of Christianity — the softer ideals of love, gentleness, tenderness, forgiveness and patience — were invoked in Africa in a manner which made the "pacification" of Africans easier and their submission to the imperial order speedier. The harder warrior values of Africa — courage, endurance, manhood, and even purposeful ruthlessness — were discouraged.

Of course Christianity in Europe itself had often sanctioned warriorhood and ruthlessness in defence of nations and tribes across centuries. But the Christianity which was being peddled in Africa in the last quarter of the nineteenth century and the first half of the twentieth was on the whole the submisive version, the version of obedience and "turning the other cheek".

We had to wait until the last third of the twentieth century to witness in Africa the re-masculation of Christianity, a readiness to invoke the macho values of militant combat in defence of justice. The World Council of Churches based in Geneva has had its debates about the legitimacy of subsidizing liberation movements in southern Africa ostensibly as a contribution to their non-military needs, though in reality it is impossible to isolate the non-military from the military in the budgets of the liberation movements.

In Nairobi I interviewed officials of the All-Africa Conference of Churches, and discussed the problems they have had with their western donors concerning the crisis about the legitimacy of violence in conditions of tyranny. Many westerners had no problem reconciling themselves to the need to help the war effort against the Nazis in the Second World War. War on that scale was of course large-scale violence. Christianity in Europe was accustomed to providing non-military support to European countries at war, be those wars defensive or aggressive. But Christians in Europe are still uncertain about providing non-military support to liberation movements waging war against racist tyrannies.

And yet the very fact that the World Council of Churches and the All-Africa Conference of Churches have defied strong lobbies against contributions to liberation movements, and have gone ahead anyhow in the task of aiding those movements, demonstrates that Christianity in Africa is undergoing the agony of change from a theology of submission to a theology of liberation. After undermining so drastically the warrior tradition in Africa in the first sixty years of the twentieth century, some Christian missions are now seeking an alliance with the warrior tradition in the liberation of southern Africa. The so-called feminine virtues of humility, forgiveness and "turning the other cheek" are being challenged by the doctrine of "using the other fist". A re-masculation of Christianity in Africa may well be under way, for better or for worse.

This brings us to the second major function of culture in society: culture as a standard of evaluation, a criterion of right and wrong, good and evil, ugly and beautiful. Inevitably this has been linked to the religious paradigm shift which has taken place. But there is also an intermingling not only with the impact of secular science on morality, but also with the impact of secular ideologies. Many Africans combine them.

Can an African be both a Christian and a Marxist? At least one major African historical figure affirmed that very clearly. Kwame Nkrumah, the first president of Ghana, declared:

"I am a Marxist-Leninist and a non-denominational Christian, and I see no contradiction in that."[3]

Can an African be both a Marxist and a Mulsim? Sékou Touré of Guinea has sometimes affirmed that. And Somalia in the 1970s has had three major historical heroes: Muhammad, Marx and the "Mad Mullah". This last was the abusive name that westerners gave to el-Haj Sayyid Muhammad Abdullah Hassan, the religious reformer and nationalist who lived from 1864 to 1920.

Can an African Muslim or Christian also belong to a traditional religion? This has clearly been a major feature of African religious experience. Millions of Muslims and Christians in the continent have managed to absorb into their systems of values and beliefs certain contributions from ancestral indigenous creeds.

Can an African be both a Christian and a Muslim? For some reason these two particular systems have tended to be in Africa, as elsewhere, mutually incompatible. A particular African family may have both Muslims and Christians. But the conscious embracing of both Christianity and Islam, the readiness of someone to call himself both a Muslim and a Christian, this is a combination still distant from the practicalities of religious synthesis.

And yet there are strong bonds between Islam and Christianity. Muslims recognize the virgin birth of Jesus but they deny his crucifixion. Christians and Muslims are therefore agreed on the beginning of Jesus's career, his birth, but not on the end, the issue of whether or not he was crucified. Muslims affirm the holiness of Jesus, but they deny his divinity. They regard him as a prophet, but not as the son of God. Christians recognize Muhammad's greatness, but they deny his holiness. They regard him as a religious genius, but not as divinely inspired.

These differences between the two systems of beliefs are as evident in Africa as elsewhere, and they do condition standards of evaluating the followers of the different religions, as well as the precepts and values involved in those religions.

Basically religious mixture is of course almost as ancient as religion itself. Certainly every Christian has, in reality, at

[3] Kwame Nkrumah, *Ghana: The Autobiography of Kwame Nkrumah* (Edinburgh and New York: Nelson, 1957).

least two religions: his own and Judaism. Every Muslim has at least three religions: his own, Christianity and Judaism. Every African Muslim has four religions: Islam, Christianity, Judaism and the legacy of his own ancestors.

All these combinations of values and beliefs have helped to make Africa a particularly fascinating theatre of cultural change, a melting pot of standards and values.

Particularly intimate are the values concerning sexuality and sex relations. We can here distinguish between pre-Christian sexual mores in Africa, Christian sexual mores and post-Christian mores.

One perennial issue is the question of polygamy in Africa. The Kenyan legislature in 1979 debated once again the issue of whether the marriage laws of the country should be standardized, and whether polygamy should either be abolished or made subject to the permission of the first wife or the prior wives. The militant machismo of Kenyan parliamentarians was staggeringly clear in the debates in the national assembly.

Of course the former president himself, Jomo Kenyatta, had not disapproved of polygamy, and had known more than one woman at a time. In his trial on charges that he had founded and managed the Mau Mau movement in the 1950s Kenyatta was explicitly asked if he approved of polygamy. He answered that he did not disapprove of it, though he would not himself call it "polygamy". The counsel for the defence, whereupon, stood up to protest that polygamy was not one of the charges being levelled against Mr Kenyatta.

What is clear is that the institution itself, though basically pre-Christian, has shown remarkable resilience even in an Africa that has been greatly influenced by Christianity. Many Africans end up having one Christian wife and more than one wife under a different traditional arrangement. When some years ago Sierra Leone's ambassador to the United Kingdom married the late President Nkrumah's former South African girl-friend, and then defended himself by saying that his prior wife at home had been married through traditional custom, the embarrassment was too great in the face of the limelight of the western press. The government of Sierra Leone, although fully aware that such things were perfectly normal in Africa, felt compelled to call back its ambassador to the United Kingdom. Since bigamy was disapproved of by the West it was regarded as too embarrassing in international diplomacy.

Then there is the whole issue of the levirate, the so-called inheriting of a wife by a surviving brother of the deceased husband. Kwame Nkrumah's mother was "inherited" by his uncle. In such cases future children of the mother are regarded as the children of the deceased husband by proxy.

When the brilliant Kenyan politician, Tom Mboya, was assassinated in a Nairobi street in 1969, his highly westernized wife, Pamela, was grief-stricken. Pamela later moved in with Mboya's brother, but not all the special customary rituals were observed, and therefore the union was not fully validated by indegenous Luo rules.

However, what was significant from our point of view was that the problem of legitimacy for the union between Tom Mboya's widow and his surviving brother arose not out of the Christian traditions in which all three had been brought up, but mainly out of the customary rituals and procedures of Luo culture to which all three belonged.

In Uganda in the early years of independence there was a combination of both royal incest in Buganda and classical polygamy all over the country. The first president of Uganda, Sir Edward Mutesa, was also the *kabaka*, or king, of Buganda. He was also supposed to be a leader of the Anglican Church of Uganda. But his sister-in-law was virtually his second wife. The son of his sister-in-law was widely regarded as the *de facto* heir to the throne. When, after Amin took over power, that son, Mutebi, was actually proclaimed Mutesa's heir, but not necessarily to the throne since the kabakaship had been abolished, the recognition seemed to have hurt Mutesa's real wife, Damali, so deeply that she turned to Catholicism for comfort. By that time Mutesa himself was dead.

Milton Obote was seen in the earlier days of independence with a woman who was regarded as his wife in traditional custom. But then Obote decided to marry outside his own ethnic community and custom. The wife was the elegant Miria, a sophisticated and westernized Muganda woman. The Christian marriage confirmed Milton Obote into Christian monogamy.

Idi Amin, being a Muslim, had fewer problems of matrimonial reconciliation between his African ancestry and the particular Middle Eastern religion he had embraced. In his first year as president he had four wives: one a Muganda, one a Musoga, one from Lango and one from the Lugbara. Amin regarded his matrimonial life as a mini-paradigm for national integration. His wives represented four different ethnic communities, he himself representing the fifth, all of them fused within the marital status of the head of state.

But Amin did something else as well. He corrected an anomaly in Ugandan law which had pretended that polygamy was a crime, when in fact it never had been for Africans in Uganda.

The legacy of Christian sex was coexisting, sometimes in fits and starts, with a pre-Christian heritage. Christianity in Africa continued to show a profound distrust of sexuality, partly derived from its own original symbolism. After all, the virgin birth of Jesus was a proclamation that the sexual act was not necessary for this being who was supposed to be the son of man as well as the son of God. The Immaculate Conception of Mary was itself part of this tendency to regard sexuality as in some sense a polluting experience.

The celibacy of Jesus Christ until he was crucified at the age of 33 was an additional affirmation. Why was this person who was supposed to be like other human beings deprived of one of the most basic of human drives, sexuality? To the present day anyone attempting to make a film in the Christian world which suggests that Jesus was human in terms of sexual instincts has immediately to confront the hostile antagonisms of believers.

Also as part of the profound Christian distrust of sexuality is the celibacy of the priesthood in the most numerous of the Christian denominations. To serve God requires a vow not just of obedience, but of sexual abstinence.

Then there is the sentence of monogamy on the rest of humankind, identifying love, perhaps too closely, with reciprocal sexual monopoly between two individuals.

The Christian distrust of sexuality in Africa included a ban by Christian missions on certain dances in schools because they were regarded as too sensuous, and on the singing of certain African songs which were regarded as too suggestive.

Now there is a post-Christian world of values as well. This is the greater liberalization of sexual behaviour in the western world. There is complete or almost complete legitimation of premarital sex all over western Europe and North America, except for small pockets of orthodoxy and traditionalism.

For many African societies a transition to premarital sex is not necessarily post-Christian, but is partly a return to the pre-Christian, the pre-colonial. There are even African societies in which a man is obliged to sleep with a woman before deciding to marry her. Sexual intercourse, far from being a prize which follows a marriage ceremony, becomes in fact part of the process of the couple getting to know each other.

Post-Christian sexual mores in the West include easier divorce. For Africa that is also part of the pre-Christian picture, where marriage was a matter of negotiation and re-negotiation, and a woman could go back to her parents either temporarily or — in the last resort — permanently, if compatibility with the husband was elusive.

In the West the post-Christian sexual revolution includes the easing of restrictions on obscenity and pornography.

In some African countries it is easier to find naked men going about their daily business in the villages than to find obscene peep shows and naked models in commercialized sexual literature in the cities.

On the contrary, some African countries have become extra puritanical about such dress as the mini-skirt. And sociologists have distinguished between nudity, which is a natural state without clothes, and nakedness, which is a state of being undressed. The latter often has sexual suggestiveness, implying focus on the vital organs.

Yet another area of post-Christian sexual mores in the West is the much greater toleration of lesbianism and male homosexuality. It is true that many Christian churches have joined in persuading western governments to relax or end laws against homosexuality, arguing that sin is a matter for the churches rather than for a state. But in reality gay liberation is an outgrowth of social liberalism, rather than a child of Christianity as such.

In Africa there are cases of women "marrying" other women, but in reality this is a different sense of marriage, and is often unrelated to sexuality. It is unisexual matrimony without homosexual intercourse.

On balance, African countries still retain strong laws against homosexuality. That is one aspect of the post-Christian sexual revolution in the West which has yet to command emulation or imitation by African governments. Africans generally enjoy more heterosexual licence in their societies than do westerners, but they enjoy less homosexual permissiveness.

What is clear is that in morality, as in law and aesthetics, Africa is in a cultural transition profoundly influencing its standards of evaluation. Parallel standards coexist in competition with each other, as the soul of Africa seeks to find an area of accommodation with competing rules of behaviour.

The third major area of function for cultures lies in motivation. Particularly important as a cultural factor is the balance between the pursuit of individual interests and the pursuit of collective welfare. In traditional African societies the scale was approximately as follows. One was first motivated to acquire enough for his or her basic needs and the needs of the immediate family. The second imperative was the pursuit of conditions to satisfy the basic needs of the wider family and society. The third imperative was the pursuit of personal advancement beyond basic needs. The fourth was the promotion of the welfare of the extended family and wider society beyond their collective needs.

Under the western impact some reshuffling of principles of behavioural motivation took place. The pursuit of basic needs still remains primary in a westernized African. But next in importance now tends to be the pursuit of self-advancement beyond basic needs. In other words, the basic needs of the wider clan are beginning to be subordinated to the imperative of personal advancement.

In some cases there is still enough surplus to enable a westernized African to contribute towards the basic needs of the extended family and clan, but that imperative is clearly on the defensive in the new conditions created by western individualism.

In the economic domain this reshuffling of drives of motivation has resulted in sharpening the profit motive. Unless restrained by a dictatorial government, an increasingly large number of African entrepreneurs have climbed the bandwagon of capitalist behaviour. Very often African enterprise lacks even the restraints that capitalism is disciplined by in its own ancestral home of the western world.

But again two systems of values are often interacting. The profit motive is partly borrowed from the West in its modern guise, but the prestige motive is part of the traditional heritage of seeking collective approval in the clan by sharing one's bounty and displaying one's cattle.

The result of this interplay between the profit motive and the prestige motive is the concurrent existence of both the motive to acquire more and more things and the motive to consume ostentatiously. To some extent this is a negation of the original Protestant ethic which is supposed to have given birth to capitalism in the West. Under the western entrepreneurial spirit, the acquisitive motive must be pronounced in the entrepreneur, but the desire to consume must be disciplined. The Calvinist ethos idealized successful acquisition in business as a potential sign of grace, but that ethos also discouraged consumption and ostentation as satans of indulgence.

But African capitalism, by combining the quest for profit with the desire for prestige, has combined in sharpening the acquisitive instinct alongside the urge to consume. Whenever possible the interest in loud and expensive cars, ostentatious dwellings, luxurious parties and entertainment, has been a concurrent feature of the drive for greater wealth in Nigeria as in Kenya, in the Ivory Coast as in Zaïre.

The fourth function of culture is as a medium of communication. This is as wide in its repercussions as culture in relation to perception. This is because how we view the world is partly a product of paradigms and perception and partly a question of conceptualization and language.

The European languages are the most important cultural bequests that Africa has received from the western world. Once again the impact of the languages on Africa has been deeper than it has been anywhere in formerly colonized Asia. Even the very identity of African countries is partly tied up with whether they speak English, French, Portuguese or some other imperial language. We never refer to "English-speaking Asia" or "French-speaking Asia" the way we refer to "anglophone Africa" and "francophone Africa". So central to the national affairs of African countries have European languages become that the languages constitute a fundamental demarcation line in the politics of the African continent and the alliances and alignments which emerge in inter-state relations.

On attainment of independence the great majority of African countries south of the Sahara chose their imperial language as the national language. They chose their members of parliament from among those of their compatriots who spoke English or French as the case might be. They similarly chose their governments from the same tiny fraction of the population which was westernized. The first great leaders of Africa until now have been disproportionately from among these westernized and semi-westernized people. They include historical giants like the late Kwame Nkrumah and contemporary giants like Julius K. Nyerere of Tanzania and Félix Houphouet-Boigny of the Ivory Coast, and fallen giants like Milton Obote of Uganda and Yakubu Gowon of Nigeria.

In my research for these Reith lectures I interviewed two reigning presidents, Léopold Senghor of Senegal and Kenneth Kaunda of Zambia. Kaunda is a striking illustration of the West's *religious* impact on Africa: he is a profoundly devout Christian. Senghor is a striking example of the West's *linguistic* impact on Africa: he is a reputable poet in the French language whose command of the language is widely respected in France itself, and who participated in drafting the present Constitution of the Fifth Republic of France. In addition, Senghor, though a champion of negritude and African values, has been in love with the French language most of his adult life. As he himself put it:

> If we had a choice we would have chosen French. Firstly, it is a language which has enjoyed a far-reaching influence and which still enjoys it in great measure. In the eighteenth century French was proposed and accepted as the universal language of culture. I know that today it comes after English, Chinese and Russian in the number of people who speak it, and it is a language of fewer countries than English. But if quantity is lacking there is quality. . . . I am not claiming that French is superior to these other languages, either in beauty or in richness, but I do say that it is the supreme language of *communication*: "a language of politeness and honesty", a language of beauty and clarity . . .[4]

Kaunda is less of a specialist in language in this poetic sense, but he is certainly in complete command of the English language as a politician and as a statesman. Senghor was the francophone

---

[4] Senghor, "Negritude and the Concept of Universal Civilisation", *Présence Africaine* (Second Quarter, 1963), Vol. 18, No. 46, p. 10.

reigning president interviewed for my Reith Lectures; Kaunda was the anglophone reigning president I interviewed.

I also interviewed a former president. This was Milton Obote of Uganda. Again the linguistic factor is important here. Obote was gracious enough to give me approximately ten hours of his time discussing a wide range of subjects. But his very identity has been affected by the English language. He would never have become president of Uganda had he not been initiated into the language of Shakespeare. And he would never have been called *"Milton"* Obote were it not for his admiration for the author of *Paradise Lost*.

Also for these Reith Lectures I interviewed the Secretary-General of the Organization of African Unity, Edem Kodjo. He is bilingual in both English and French. But for our discussion here it is worth noting that his credentials for the job as Secretary-General of the Organization of African Unity required, among other qualifications, precisely that competence in both English and French. The business of pan-Africanism is difficult enough as it is; it would be doubly compounded if the Secretary-General were unilingual.

I also interviewed Adebayo Adedeji, who heads the United Nations Economic Commission for Africa. Adedeji is a distinguished economist. But his qualifications as an economist could not have been transmitted to him in any of the indigenous Nigerian languages. Highly skilled economists in contemporary Africa are inevitably products of training in a European language, usually the language of the country's own previous imperial ruler.

I also discussed some of the themes of these lectures with African intellectuals of Marxist persuasion. For the time being it is a socio-linguistic impossibility for an African to be a sophisticated Marxist without at the same time being substantially westernized. This is because the works of Karl Marx, and the enormous body of commentary on those works, are not yet available in indigenous African languages except for a few specimens in Swahili, Amharic and one or two other key languages.

For an African to be sophisticated enough to read Marx's *Capital* he must have not merely a knowledge of a European language, but an impressive command of that language. Even those Africans who are first exposed to Marxism by studying in the Soviet Union find their way to the Soviet Union initially through a western European language. No Africans are ever admitted to Soviet universities directly from some village compound. The young men and women are first exposed to primary and secondary schools in the western tradition before they can be expected to make head or tail of the curriculum of, for example, Patrice Lumumba University in Moscow.

It is because of these considerations that African Marxists are inevitably, and of necessity, products initially of western education and western linguistic competence.

This has in fact taken us into the fifth function of culture in society, culture as a basis of stratification. There is little doubt that western culture has helped to redefine the pecking order in African societies.

In my writings I have sometimes described the intelligentsia in Africa as an educated *class*, partly because I have been convinced that, whatever Karl Marx might have surmised about the role of economic factors in class formation in nineteenth-century Europe, class formation in twentieth-century Africa has been profoundly affected by western education. The colonial impact, I have argued, transformed the natural basis of stratification in Africa. Instead of status based on, say, age, there emerged status based on literacy. Instead of classes emerging from the question, "Who owns what?", class formation now responds to the question, "Who knows what?" The knowledge may indeed be merely literary, but the colonial impact certainly distorted reality both in a Marxist materialist sense and in an African normative sense. The very process of acquiring aspects of the imperial culture came to open the doors first of influence, and later of affluence itself.[4]

Two forms of knowledge have been particularly critical in determining who rules Africa: literary of academic knowledge among African intellectuals and military knowledge within the African armed forces. The knowledge of the intelligentsia has produced something approaching a *meritocracy*; the skills of the soldiers have produced what might be called a *militocracy*.

[5] This thesis is argued out more fully in Mazrui, *Political Values and the Educated Class in Africa* (London: Heinemann Educational Books; Berkeley and Los Angeles: University of California Press, 1978).

In politics in Africa the pendulum sometimes swings between a meritocratic elite this year and a militocracy following a coup next year. The African intelligentsia is in command of western verbal and literary skills; the African soldiers are trying to be in command of western military know-how.

To take one example, Milton Obote, an African intellectual if ever there was one, was overthrown by a soldier called Idi Amin in January 1971. In the neighbouring country of Tanzania, Julius Nyere, another African intellectual, engaged first in a verbal war with Idi Amin, and then let loose his own soldiers on Amin's army and drove Amin from power.

But who succeeded Amin in Uganda initially? A band of intellectuals and academics, all highly westernized. Indeed, the first president after Idi Amin was a former vice-chancellor of a western-style university, Makerere. When former Vice-Chancellor Lule was ousted from power, he was succeeded by Her Majesty Queen Elizabeth's Counsel, Godfrey Binaisa, Q.C. The rest of the top political establishment of post-Amin Uganda included a number of Ugandans who had just scrambled back home from university jobs elsewhere in Africa or in the western world. The Ugandan case has been a classic instance of the pendulum between meritocracy and militocracy.

The situation in Ghana has also been comparable from that point of view. Kwame Nkrumah, a highly articulate African intellectual, was overthrown by soldiers. When the soldiers stepped down, an academic called Kafi Busia succeeded. He in turn was overthrown by soldiers in 1972. Those soldiers had their own internal palace coups until finally the decision was made in 1979 to hand over to civilians. Again the civilians were within the tradition of Africa's westernized intelligentzia. Hilla Limann, a former Foreign Service officer, defeated Victor Owusu for the presidency. The soldiers were still in power when the elections took place, and some of the worst political atrocities of independent Ghana were committed during that period when three former heads of state were arbitrarily executed. The tension within the armed forces cast its shadow over prospects for the restoration of a civilian meritocracy. But behind both forms of rule in Africa is western culture, either literary and verbal, producing the Nkrumahs and the Busias, or military, with products like Achiampong and Flight-Lieutenant Rawlings. Western culture has once again conditioned Africa's political stratification.

As for the role of culture in production and distribution, we are treating these economic aspects more fully in other lectures. Western systems of production and distribution carry with them cultural implications. Consumption patterns change in the wake of canned fruit and a newly-assembled bicycle. New skills are transmitted through the activities of western transnational corporations. The creation of new types of jobs in turn transforms the nature of individual ambition and occupational aspirations. The urban bias in African development induces migration from the rural areas to the urban centres with further modifications in cultural patterns of life. Capitalism itself erodes aspects of African traditional fellowship and collective life. The money economy has created new ambitions of accumulation of surplus and the construction of commercial empires. A new juju has cast its spell, mesmerizing the ambitious, titillating the greedy, spellbinding the acquisitive. The new juju is cold foreign exchange, the availability of convertible currency as a form of international power. We shall return to some of these monetary and economic issues in subsequent lectures. Suffice it here to say that economic forces and processes of production are a fundamental aspect of Africa's assimilation not only into the world economy, but also into western culture.

Finally, we have the seventh function of culture in society: the function of identity. Culture does help to define the "we" and "they" in given situations.

The effect of western culture on different levels of identity in Africa has not always been intentional. For example, the process of incorporating several linguistic and ethnic groups into one new political community called, say, Nigeria, helped to sharpen the consciousness of ethnic identities in that shared arena of competition, and created new regional loyalties and allegiances. Some scholars have argued that it is not merely the new nation states which have been created by western colonialism; it is also the phenomenon of "tribalism". Some groups in Africa did not realize they were a particular ethnic community until relatively recently. This followed western policies of "tribal reserves" and the whole paradigm of looking at people in ethnic terms.

Also a product of Africa's interaction with Europe is the whole problem of race consciousness. The cross of humiliation which Africa has had to carry through the centuries, partly based on European racism and cultural arrogance, has played a part in making Africans see themselves as black people. This helped to deepen racial solidarity to such an extent that by the time southern Africa was struggling for its liberation, it could count on considerable support from the rest of the continent.

But race consciousness has of course its hazards, as well as its strengths. Its tragedies in recent African history have included the expulsion of people of Asian origin from Uganda by Idi Amin in 1972, and the murder of innocent missionaries in southern Africa in the wake of the unfolding racial conflict.

On balance, the three most basic levels of identity that the western impact has deepened among Africans are first the identity of "tribe" as the different groups have competed for scarce resources in new territories created by the West; secondly, there is the identity of the nation state as Africans go about calling themselves Nigerians or Kenyans as a result of boundaries created by the colonial power; and thirdly, the identity of race, which has in part been a reaction to European chauvinism and arrogance towards non-white people in the last few centuries.

But in addition to these three levels of identity — "tribal", national and racial — it is arguable that even the identity of an individual as a distinct personality has been deepened by the impact of western liberal thought with its principles of individualism and personal accountability. It is arguable that western forms of individualism emerged partly out of the impact of Christianity, especially its Protestant versions. Ideas of personal accountability before God, reinforced by individual choice between good and evil, contributed to the emerging forces of individualism in Africa.

Alongside Christianity was western liberalism itself with its notions of "one man, one vote" and its emphasis on the right to privacy and personal choice in matters which range from the ballot to the boudoir. Ideas of John Stuart Mill, Thomas Jefferson and Jean-Jacques Rouseau inspired African doctrines of liberty in both the collective sense of national self-determination and in the personal sense of individual freedom.

After Christianity and liberalism as generators of individual thought there was also the rising trend of urbanization. The migration from the countryside to the cities was in part a transition from the constraints of collective village life to the relative permissiveness of urban life.

The fourth force which has generated individualism in Africa is western capitalism. We have referred already to concepts like the profit motive and private enterprise in connection with changing patterns of behaviour and motivation. But free enterprise is a combination of corporate organization and private shareholding. The pursuit of personal profit has escalated in African economic systems. This is both a reflection and a reinforcement of the growing trend towards individualism.

Many aspects of life are changed as a result. To marry primarily for love rather than for the collective welfare of the family or clan is itself a matter of individualism in matters of marriage. Monogamy is a slogan of "one man, one wife", echoing the electoral cry of "one man, one vote". The money economy has made wives more expensive, and has therefore discouraged polygamy. Wife labour may be all right for subsistence agriculture but not for urban industry.

Wage labour is also in part a case of rewarding men in precise monetary terms for their continuation as individual workers. Very often the very hours of work are counted, a procedure which takes a newly arrived rural "boy" a little while to understand when he gets his first job in town. The money economy and the culture of the clock have introduced new and more precise measurements of individual effort.

The fifth force which has generated individualism consists of the rules of western education and science. To get help in writing your essay at school could be a case of cheating, certainly copying from your friend in an examination is a great violation of the code of honour. One is judged in an examination as an *individual*.

Higher up the educational ladder is the Ph.D. thesis which is supposed to be not only individually distinctive but also original. As an individual scholar the candidate is supposed to say something that nobody else has said before, often a case of individualism gone mad.

Scientific discoveries are carefully attributed to individuals like Darwin, Einstein and smaller fry.

Then there are the rules of western art. Plagiarism can be a serious intellectual and artistic sin. Had Shakespeare been

writing in the twentieth century, he would have been taken
to court by several publishers for plagiarising or pirating the
works of others. Since his day the rules of scholarship and
creativity in the western world have become more rigidly
individualistic and less collective than they were for the Eliza-
bethans.

Yet in Africa the oral tradition is still a case of cumulative
collective wisdom. Oral literature is often a literature without
authors: ballads and folk tales recited down the generations
without specific attribution as to who first composed or in-
vented them. Tunes from drums, flutes and xylophones cannot
be traced to individual great composers of the past.

Christianity, western liberal democracy, urbanization, western
capitalism, the rules of western science and the rules of western
art have jointly exerted an unparalleled influence on the emergence of personalized identity in Africa.

What emerges from all this is that the African has discovered
himself as an individual, and a black man, and as a citizen of a
particular modern African country, and indeed as a resident
within the African continent, partly because of his historical
interaction with western culture in all its richness and all its
narrowness, in all its conquering aggressiveness.

These then are the seven functions of culture in society and
the extent to which they have been influenced by the cultural
penetration of the West into the souls of African people.

For the Third World as a whole one lesson in the future is
the gradual counterpenetration of the West by the Third World.
That is one reason why I have been fascinated by the missionary
activities in the United States of the Reverend Sun Myung
Moon of the Unification Church. In fact, partly intrigued by
this phenomenon of a Korean defiantly acting as a missionary
in the heartland of the western world, I have attempted to
follow the Unification Church. I have in fact been attending
the International Conferences on the Unity of the Sciences
since 1975. These conferences are sponsored by the International Cultural Foundation in New York, which has in turn
been funded partly by the Reverend Moon.

Many American parents are incensed that their children
have flocked to this movement. I can understand the feelings
of parents who regard a religious leader as a rival. I am sure
I would be similarly jealous of a religious leader who threatened

my rights as a parent in terms of the loyalty and fidelity of my children. I have three sons of my own. But I happen also to be an African, and I know that my sons would be similarly exposed to the blandishments of missionaries had I still been living in Africa. The only difference in Africa is that the missionaries would have been western, belonging to such established denominations as Methodism of Catholicism, for example. Is missionary activity in America by the Unification Church any different from missionary activity in Africa by Catholic, Methodist or Anglican churches? Is the rigid discipline imposed by Reverend Moon any different from the rigid discipline imposed on African children by Christian disciplinarians in the villages of Zaire or Upper Volta?

In fact, as an African, I cannot help admiring Koreans for giving Americans a taste of their own medicine. The Korean Central Intelligence Agency has done to some American politicians what the American CIA has always attempted to do to politicians in the Third World: buy them out, bribe them, subvert them or threaten them. I personally am delighted that the Korean CIA has by implication begun to teach Americans the modified golden rule, "Do not do unto others what you would not that they do unto you".

As I shall explain more fully in a subsequent lecture, I believe in *counterpenetrating* the citadels of power in the West. Economically this is done when OPEC buys shares in major western industries. Intellectually this is partly achieved when teachers from the Third World begin to teach and influence young westerners the way western teachers have for long sought to mould the minds of young Africans and Asians. Religiously, counterpenetration is partly achieved when missionaries from Asia and Africa begin to preach and proselytize in western countries. Reverend Moon, with all his faults, may be part of the vanguard of religious counterpenetration into the citadels of western Christendom.

The struggle against Western religious subculture and supremacy is likely to be slow. But interdependence is not merely an economic condition; it has also to become a cultural relationship. The western world has to experience a new paradigm shift, a shift in the direction of cultural humility, a readiness to be influenced by others and a willingness to help construct a new and more balanced international cultural order.

LECTURE 4

The Burden of Underdevelopment

Until the 1970s the terms "poor countries" and "underdeveloped countries" were virtually interchangeable. Clearly countries like South Yemen or Tanzania were both poor and underdeveloped.

But the emergence of oil power has shattered this easy equation. Virtually all Third World countries are still technically underdeveloped, but only some of them are now poor. South Yemen and Tanzania are still good illustrations of the old equation. They are both poor and underdeveloped. But in the 1970s it has become difficult to think of Saudi Arabia as a poor country. On the contrary, this is one of the best endowed countries in the world in oil-wealth and dollar reserves, while being at the same time one of the least developed.

What is true of Saudi Arabia as a country is substantially true of Africa as a continent. In terms of resources, Africa is one of the best endowed regions of the world, but it is still the least developed of the inhabited continents. This is *the pathology of technical backwardness*.

A related paradox is that, per head of each group's population, the richest inhabitants of Africa are non-Africans. The poorest in per capita terms are indigenous Africans themselves. That is one reason why the highest standards of living are among white people in southern Africa.

Of course, there are rich blacks as well as rich whites in the continent. But again, we find that there are more white millionaires per head of the white population of the continent than there are black millionaires in relation to numbers of blacks around. This is *the pathology of maldistribution*.

The third interrelated paradox is that while the continent as a whole is, as indicated, rich in resources, it is so fragmented that it includes the majority of the poorest nations of the world. The paradox here is of a rich continent which contains many poverty-stricken societies. This is *the pathology of a fragmented economy.*

Let us look at this paradox of a rich Africa inhabited by underprivileged Africans.

Estimates of Africa's resources are on the whole tentative. Not enough prospecting for resources under the ground has taken place, but it is already fair to say that Africa has 96 per cent of the non-Communist world's diamonds, 60 per cent of its gold, 42 per cent of its cobalt, 34 per cent of its bauxite and 28 per cent of its uranium.

Africa's iron reserves are probably twice those of the United States, and its reserves of chrome are the most important by far outside the Soviet Union.

In the 1970s the United States has been importing 98 per cent of its manganese from abroad, nearly half of which has been from Africa.

The West's interest in Africa's oil has also significantly increased, partly in proportion to the political uncertainties surrounding the Middle Eastern suppliers. Had Nigeria joined the Arab oil embargo of the United States in 1973, the consequences for America would have been severe. In 1974, the year following the embargo, the United States' balance of payments deficit with Nigeria was already $3 billion. It rose to $5 billion two years later. For the time being America's dependence on Nigerian oil continues to be critical.

Then there is Africa's agricultural potential. The Republic of Sudan, Africa's largest country in square miles, may indeed develop into a major bread-basket for parts of Africa and the Middle East before the end of the century. More effective irrigation would facilitate full exploitation of the impressive fertility of this part of the continent.

Then there are Africa's water resources, with some of the greatest rivers of the world. Potentialities for building dams and generating hydro-electric power have only just begun to be exploited.

Solar energy for domestic and public purposes is still in its infancy. But it should be remembered that Africa is the most exposed of all continents to the sun. The Equator cuts Africa right in the middle. And Africa is the only continent which is cut by both the Tropic of Cancer and the Tropic of Capricorn. Tapping solar energy in Africa, once the technique becomes sophisticated, could be an additional impressive source of power and energy.

With regard to uranium, Africa's resources may be significantly greater than at present estimated. One country that became a uranium-producing state fairly recently is Niger, formerly a French colony.

Against the background of mineral, agricultural and other resources in Africa there is also the disconcerting fact that Africa has some of the least developed countries in the world. The overwhelming majority of the countries that the United Nations regards as the "poorest" in the world are in fact in Africa. They range from Upper Volta to Rwanda and Burundi and from Somalia to Tanzania.

The continent itself seems to be well endowed with resources, but a disproportionate number of people in the population of the continent is undernourished and underprivileged. A situation where a continent is well-endowed but the people are poor is a situation of anomalous underdevelopment.

A substantial part of the explanation lies in the nature of Africa's economic interaction with the western world across time. Trade is the oldest of the different areas of economic interaction, foreign investment being relatively recent. Trade between Europe and Africa goes back to the slave trade and the traffic in firearms and later in primary commodities.

The agricultural potentialities of Africa were realized quite early, though they continue to be under-utilized. As a western historian put it back in 1879, Africa contained

> millions of square miles of rich and fertile lands, some of which are open and parklike in their appearance; and others covered with extensive forests of valuable timber, where the sound of the woodman's axe has never yet been heard, and which only require the culture of the husbandman to make them produce an ample return for labour.[1]

[1] Cited by Robin Hallett, "Changing European attitudes to Africa", in John E. Flint (ed.) *Cambridge History of Africa*, Vol. 5 (Cambridge: Cambridge University Press, 1977), p. 486.

But the fertile land was accompanied in some cases by a harsh climate for the European and sometimes even for the local inhabitants. The mosquito and the tse-tse fly took their toll.

It was not until the last quarter of the nineteenth century that an entirely new potential source of wealth began to be taken seriously. As the same writer has put it:

> By 1875 the discovery of diamonds in South Africa had provided a striking indication of the entirely unexpected riches to be found in Africa, and given new meaning to the wise remark made by Samuel Parchas more than two hundred years earlier: "And yet may Africa have a Prerogative in Rarities, and some seeming Incredibilities be true".[2]

But in fact much of British investment for more than half a century went to South Africa. Up to 1936 South Africa received nearly half of Africa's total capital inflow from outside. In the rest of Africa there was in the initial phases a relatively heavy proportion of infrastructural investment.

The period of perhaps greatest railway building activity was from 1890 to 1914. Some of the railway lines which were built had no immediate prospects, but were truly a kind of investment in the future. The railway line from Mombasa in Kenya to the lakes in the interior of East Africa was built between 1896 and 1901. At the time it was widely regarded as a lunatic venture, a white elephant in a dark continent with a gloomy future. But in fact the railway line came to serve Kenya and Uganda exceptionally well. There was considerable talk in western circles at the time about a possible Cape-to-Cairo railway line. Unfortunately that transcontinental dream never materialized.

In subsequent years there was also investment in Africa's sources of power and energy. Africa may have nearly 30 per cent of the world's potential for hydro-electric power. Some moves towards tapping these immense resources were made, especially after the Second World War. The Owen Falls dam across the Nile in Uganda generates power for Uganda itself and for about a third of Kenya's needs. The Volta River project in Ghana was later linked to aluminium smelting, and could be

[2] Ibid., p. 487.

part of the basis of further development in Ghana when some of the other economic problems of the country are transcended.

The Second World War was an important divide in Africa's developmental experience. There is widespread consensus that the war definitely contributed towards Africa's *political* liberation. It did this partly by undermining western Europe's capacity to hold on to empires. Britain was exhausted and substantially impoverished by the time the war ended. France had been humiliated in defeat at the hands of the Germans.

Related to the exhaustion and impoverishment of western Europe following its own fratricidal war was the destruction of the myth of European invincibility in the eyes of the colonized peoples. Suddenly somebody noticed in Bombay that the emperor's new clothes of modern technology were not clothes at all — the British Raj was naked! And when the Indians started pointing fingers and exposing the nakedness of their emperor, other subject peoples elsewhere saw it too. That is one reason why the precedent set by India in challenging British rule became an important inspiration to many African nationalists.

At a more individual level the war also cut the white man down to size in African eyes. The colonial situation until then cried out loud for two processes of humanization. The colonized Africans had had their humanity reduced partly because they were regarded as part devils and part monkeys. They certainly had their adulthood reduced when they were often equated with children. As I was growing up in Mombasa in the 1940s, the film censors declared some films as being "not suitable for Africans and children under 16". And since the population of Mombasa was in part racially mixed, and many Arabs looked like Africans, there were two kinds of identification tests at the door of the Regal Cinema in Mombasa. An African who wanted desperately to see the particular film could try and convince the ticket clerk that he was really an Arab. Secondly, the fifteen-year-old who was desperate to see the film had to convince the clerk that he was really sixteen. This equation of Africanness with childhood began to be undermined as a result of war experiences and the role of African soldiers in combat as brave and determined adults.

On the other hand, Europeans had been portrayed as super-adult and virtually super-human. The war in turn humanized white men in the eyes of their African colleagues as they fought together in the Horn of Africa, in North Africa, in places like Malaya and elsewhere. To witness a white man scared to death under fire was itself a revelation to many Africans who had previously seen white men only in their arrogant commanding postures as a colonial élite.

So, while the image of the African was humanized by being pulled up from equation with devils, monkeys and children, the image of the white man was humanized by being pulled down from equation with supermen, angels and the gods themselves.

The third effect of the war was to broaden the general social and political horizons not only of ex-servicemen who had served in the war, but of many Africans who had remained behind. The idea of listening to the radio for *overseas* news concerning the war gathered momentum during the war. Individual Africans in a township were, in terms of conversations among themselves, identified as being either pro-British or pro-German. My father, for his sins, was pro-British and I remember long debates he used to have with his friends in a relaxed mood debating the significance of the latest news item about the war abroad, and whether it was good news or bad news for the different fans of the British on one side and the Germans on the other. I was a child then listening with rapture to this kind of exchange. It was clear that the grownups regarded the contending forces in Europe partly as soccer teams writ large, and the Africans were placing their bets on the two European powers at war with each other. We should remember that East Africa had once known both German rule in Tanganyika, Rwanda and Burundi, and British rule in Uganda and Kenya. The two colonial and former colonial powers at war with each other were ominous masters, and yet also frivolous soccer teams in deadly rivalry with each other.

But the very tendency of my father and his friends to debate the progress of the war almost as if it were the progress of a football match increased their interest in world affairs and broadened their vision of human possibilities. For millions of Africans all over the continent the Second World War was an important internationalizing experience. By the end of it many Africans were ready to agitate for freedom and independence.

The Second World War was also liberating for Africa because at the end of it the pinnacle of world power was no longer in western Europe but had divided itself between Washington and Moscow. The two superpowers both had a tradition of anti-imperialism in at least some sense, though both superpowers are also guilty of other forms of imperialism. What is clear is that the rise of the Soviet Union and the pre-eminence of the United States after the Second World War created two pressures on European powers to make concessions to African nationalists struggling for independence. The West's fear of the Soviet Union sometimes retarded the process of liberation, but in the end facilitated that process, convincing westerners that it was a good idea to give independence to moderate Africans while there was still time and avert the threat of radicalizing Africans still further and driving them into the hands of the Soviet Union.

But although the Second World War was indeed politically liberating for Africans in the sense that we have mentioned, that same war was an important stage in the incorporation of Africa into the world capitalist system. Partly in pursuit of war needs, African agriculture was modified to produce urgently needed supplies and food for Europe at war. In some parts of Africa there was a major depression later when the war demand for African-produced goods declined, but the structure of African agriculture had by then already entered a new phase of export bias. The trend towards slanting African agriculture in this direction continued unabated.

Some of the postwar schemes for African development initiated by the colonial powers were indeed failures. One of the most spectacular of the failures was the groundnut scheme in Tanganyika, flamboyantly conceived in terms of large-scale groundnut development, and deemed to be an appropriate strategy of interdependence between Africa and Europe. The scheme was designed to help supply Europe with certain food oils while generating development in Africa. As it turned out, the scheme was ill conceived, badly located, and disastrously implemented by the British authorities in East Africa.

But on balance the principle of developing African agriculture to serve European needs was quite well entrenched. The war had helped to consolidate it.

Another way in which the war created the foundations of further economic dependency lay in the manner in which it helped to transform colonial policy from the morality of maintaining law and order in Africa (*Pax Britannica*) to a new imperial morality of increasing development in the colonies and pursuing the welfare of the colonized peoples. Britain established the Colonial Development and Welfare Fund as part of the machinery of this new imperial vision. It was not enough to stop Africans fighting each other; it was not enough to control cattle raids between different communities and tribes; it was not enough to make an example of political agitators in order to maintain the mystique of *Pax Britannica*; it was not enough to use the slogan of law and order; imperial power was a kind of trust, a mandate to serve the subject peoples.

The vision itself was of course much older than the Second World War. It was even explicit in Rudyard Kipling's notorious poem "The White Man's Burden" first published in *The Times* on 4 February 1899.

> Take up the white man's burden —
> Send forth the best ye breed —
> Go bind your sons to exile
> To serve your captive's need.
> To wait in heavy harness,
> On flattered folk and wild —
> Your new caught, sullen peoples,
> Half-devil and half-child.
> . . . .
> Take up the white man's burden —
> The savage wars of peace —
> Fill full the mouth of Famine
> And bid the sickness cease;
> . . . .
> Take up the white man's burden —
> No tawdry rule of kings,
> But toil of serf and sweeper —
> The tale of common things.
> The ports ye shall not enter,
> The roads ye shall not tread,
> Go make them with your living,
> And mark them with your dead.

The developmental imperative of service was certainly very explicit in this poem. But on balance it was not in fact until the Second World War that development as a major imperative of colonial policy became a genuine exertion. New projects for rural development were more systematically implemented, and new trends in educational policy were soon discernible. Virtually all the major universities in black Africa were established after the Second World War, many of them soon after the war in response to the new developmental imperative in colonial policy.

But these thrusts of development were themselves a further aggravation of Africa's incorporation into western capitalism. The Colonial Development and Welfare Fund contributed in its own way towards deepening both Africa's economic dependency on the West and Africa's cultural imitation of the West.

Important biases in the direction of development included, first, the export bias we have just mentioned. Cash crops for export were given priority as against food for local people. One-quarter to one-third of the total cultivated areas in some of the more fertile colonies were devoted to the production of such export commodities as cocoa in Ghana, coffee in Uganda, groundnuts in Senegal and The Gambia, pyrethrum in Tanganyika and tea in Kenya.

Another distortion which occurred in the development process was the urban bias. Much of the economic change internally subordinated the needs of the countryside to the needs of the towns. One consequence was the volume of migration from rural areas to urban centres. The crisis of habitability continued to beset the lot of the country folk. Young men struggled for a while, then downed their tools, and hit the high road towards the uncertain fortunes of the capital city.

A third bias within each country was the subregional distortion. Some parts of the country were just much more developed than others. This burden of uneven development had its own stresses and strains. By being more developed than its neighbours the Buganda subregion of Uganda, for example, acquired not only extra leverage, but also the passionate jealousies and distrust of other parts of the country. With less than one-fifth of the population of Uganda, Buganda held sway and exercised undue leverage over the political and economic destiny of the country as a whole. Uganda is now very difficult to govern with the help of the Buganda, and very difficult to govern without their help. The chronic instability of Uganda is partly the result of ethnic confrontations and partly the outcome of uneven development among the different subregions and groups in the country.

The fourth distortion in the history of development in Africa was the distortion which occurred in parts of the continent settled and, at least for a while, controlled by whites. In 1938, out of a total of £1,222 million capital invested in Africa no less than £555 million was invested in South Africa from outside. A further £102 million was invested in Rhodesia. These countries under white settler control acquired in addition considerable economic muscle in their own parts of the continent, with leverage over their neighbours. Rhodesia exercised economic influence over Zambia, Malawi, Botswana and Mozambique.

Kenya, while it was still a colonial territory, exercised considerable economic influence on the neighbouring countries of Tanganyika, Uganda and Zanzibar. South Africa itself is now basically a giant in the southern African subcontinent with considerable potential for buying friends or neutralizing enemies.

The fifth bias in Africa's development takes us back to capitalism. For in this case we are indeed dealing with the capitalist bias in Africa's recent economic history: absorption into international structures of trade and capital flow, belief in the efficacy of market forces, faith in the profit motive and private enterprise, distrust of state initiatives in the economy, and optimism about the developmental value of foreign investments.

It is partly the nature of these five biases in the history of economic change in the continent that has condemned the continent to the paradox of retardation: a continent well endowed in mineral wealth and agricultural potential which is at the same time a continent of the countries which the United Nations has calculated to be the poorest in the world.

The question which arises is what is to be done to help Africa to transcend this predicament of retardation? Can Africa modernize without westernizing?

My own definition of modernization is change in the direction which is compatible with the present stage of human knowledge, and which does justice to the human person as an innovative and social being.

If a society does not want to take into account present-day

levels of knowledge, science and scholarship, that society is pre-modern.

If a society suppresses innovativeness, and insists on doing things according only to tradition, that society is pre-modern.

If a society interprets the concept of man as a social being too narrowly, limiting social loyalties to clans and tribes or even just to nations, turns its back on the outer world of fellow human beings, that society is still pre-modern.

If modernity is defined according to these three basic principles of responsiveness to the highest levels of knowledge, encouragement of innovation, and enlargement of social sympathies, there are clearly different roads to modernity.

For the Third World the best way of modernizing without westernizing is, on the one side, to adopt those three principles of modernity that I have mentioned and, on the other, to pursue strategies of decolonization and of reducing dependency. What is needed is a dual effort to modernize and decolonize at the same time — it is an effort to decolonize modernity.

Given those three principles of the modern approach, how do we marry them to strategies of decolonization and liberation?

I myself would recommend seven strategies of liberation. The first is to some extent already under way. This is the strategy of indigenization of personnel, as programmes for the Africanization of administration, management, clerical manpower and the like have got under way. This use of indigenous human resources is certainly an important aspect. In the southern African situation the increased use of indigenous personnel in different areas of economic activity will in turn prove to be the Achilles heel of the racially-based economic system, undermining its very foundations. But elsewhere in Africa, there is a danger that the indigenization of personnel is merely window-dressing; substituting black faces in the front for white faces, but maintaining a system of dependency and distortion all the same.

In spite of these reservations, there is no escaping the necessity of increased utilization of indigenous human resources as part of this first strategy of liberation.

Also fundamental to the strategy of indigenization is the need to develop further indigenous resources as against relying on imports where this option is open. Greater utilization of hydro-electric power, for example, would sometimes reduce dependence on imported coal or oil.

Greater utilization of indigenous technology and know-how must also be mentioned. The struggle for simpler forms of technology is part of the process of reducing reliance on outsiders for sophisticated know-how. In recent times there has even been increased interest in traditional African medicine with special reference to some of the herbs which were used in therapy. Experience was the medical school of precolonial African doctors and medicine men. Some of these herbs, under modern chemical analysis, have yielded important information on their medicinal values.

In terms of the African economy as a whole, there is also the slow process of attempting to indigenize control and decision-making in major industries and firms. Nigeria has been moving in that direction in the 1970s. The Ivory Coast, on the other hand, continues to rely disproportionately on French personnel and advisers for areas of economic activity which in many other parts of Africa have long been under indigenous control.

My second strategy for transcending dependency is the strategy of domestication. This is different from indigenization. Domestication involves making a resource which is foreign more relevant and more appropriate for the African situation. For example, the African university today is basically a foreign institution, transmitting foreign culture and techniques, consolidating foreign academic traditions, and even preparing the way for foreign ideologies among students and future teachers. Domesticating the African university would involve making it more relevant to local needs, and more responsive to branches of knowledge and understanding available elsewhere on the local scene. The teaching of African history instead of British imperial history at Makerere University was a modest venture in the domestication of the Department of History.

Parliament in Nairobi is in conception a foreign institution. It has all the paraphernalia of Parliament at Westminster without the sanctity of tradition and stamp of authority. Budget Day is very much like Budget Day at Westminster, with the black briefcase of Kenya's equivalent of the Chancellor of the Exchequer. The speaker wears regalia reminiscent of the speaker of the House of Commons. And for more than a decade after independence the language of discussion in Kenya's National

Assembly was exclusively English.

But when the late President Kenyatta ordered that deliberations in the Kenyan Parliament were from 1974 to be in Kiswahili, this was a major stage in the domestication of the parliamentary institution in Kenya. Anomalies have remained. The language of debate is indeed Kiswahili, but the laws come before Parliament couched in the English language. The official language of the constitution when it is being interpreted in the law courts is English, but the basic language of national politics is Kiswahili. Domesticating the political system, borrowed from a liberal democratic tradition from outside, has necessitated its own Swahilization.

Domesticating the economy itself involves a reduction of its export orientation, and an enhancement of the focus on domestic food needs and other local requirements.

Sometimes emphasizing labour-intensive instead of capital-intensive technology is itself a form of domesticating the techniques of production, distribution, communication and exchange. Labour-intensive technology is a form of democratizing modernity, involving more and more people in the process of modern production, and utilizing a major resource of even the poorest of the African countries – the human resource.

My third strategy for transcending dependency is the strategy of diversification. I start from the premise that there are occasions when freedom begins with the multiplication of one's masters. If one is owned and controlled by only one power, freedom is often particularly restrictive. But if an African society cultivates the skills to have more than one hegemonic power competing for it, this has possibilities for liberation. To be dependent on two giants, especially when the giants have rivalries between them, is sometimes an opportunity to play one against the other – and maximize one's own options.

African societies must therefore diversify and sometimes multiply their trading partners. This at times may require that they also diversify what they produce, avoiding predicaments of excessive dependence on one or two commodities.

Thirdly, there is the need to diversify one's investors. French-speaking countries tend to be excessively preoccupied with facilitating French investment. To that extent their freedom of manoeuvre is more restricted than among those English-speaking countries that have already moved beyond their original metropole and cultivated new potential western risk-takers to invest in their societies.

Fourthly, there is the need to diversify one's aid donors. Many of these aid donors insist on bilateral aid between the giver and the receiver, but new aid institutions have grown up, such as the Arab Bank for African Development. Indeed, the emergence of oil-rich members of the Organization of Petroleum-Exporting Countries has introduced a qualitative stage in the diversification of potential aid donors for African countries. In relation to gross national product, the OPEC countries give a higher percentage of aid than do western countries. But there is clearly no room for complacency, especially since OPEC is also responsible for new and sometimes crippling oil prices. Nevertheless, the rise of OPEC to new levels of power has been one of the most important and healthiest developments of the 1970s, as we shall later elaborate.

There are other areas of diversification which Africans need to explore, including exposing themselves to a wider range of foreign cultural influences than they have done so far. To be exposed only to the western cultural impact creates a deeper condition of dependency than to be exposed to a variety of influences from Canada to India, from Germany to China, from Japan to the Soviet Union.

Ideologically, Africa also needs to diversify its options. Closed ideological systems perpetrate mental and intellectual dependency. African societies should be open enough to let contending ideological forces compete for leverage. Thus western individualism, Marxist class concepts, Gandhian ideas of compromise and the indigenous values underpinning African cultures themselves can be let loose on the free market of ideas.

My fourth strategy for transcending dependency is a strategy which I call, in my own jargon, horizontal interpenetration. By this I mean the capacity of developing countries themselves to interpenetrate each other in trade, investment, aid and other forms of contact. Until now the bulk of the trade of the world goes on between the rich industrialized countries of the northern hemisphere (north–north trade). Second in importance is the economic interaction between the northern hemisphere and the developing countries of the Third World (north–south trade and the like). Only thirdly in importance is trade and investment and aid among developing countries themselves (south–south economic interaction).

What is required is greater cooperation, contact and inter-action among African countries themselves and between African countries and countries of Asia and Latin America. Cases of horizontal interpenetration include Egypt's and India's export of manpower to other developing countries, the Arab world's aid to African and Asian countries, and Cuba's military assistance to Angola, Ethiopia and other African countries. All these are cases where the resources of one Third World country are made available for specific purposes to serve the needs of another Third World country. The acceleration of this trend is an important aspect of the whole struggle against dependency.

My fifth strategy for transcending these economic handicaps is the strategy of what I call vertical counterpenetration into the citadels of power. Under this strategy the aim is to increase the share of the Third World in the economies of the developed industrial nations themselves, and therefore enhance Third World leverage over those economies. The beginnings of counter-penetration lie in the psychological discovery that the resources of Third World societies are not necessarily merely a basis of dependency on the western world, but could be converted into power over the western world. For decades oil in the Middle East was one additional reason why the oil producers were controlled by others. And then a number of countries formed a producers' cartel called the Organization of Petroleum-Exporting Countries, and before very long a resource which had caused its possessors to be subjugated became a weapon of the possessors capable of being wielded against the imperial powers that had once dominated them.

Of course oil is an exceptional case in terms of its potential for use against the industrial nations. But my generalization is still correct, that the spirit of counterpenetration by the Third World into the northern hemisphere must begin with a re-evaluation by Third World societies on how best to utilize their own resources to maximize international leverage. At least as important is the need for Third World countries, in-cluding members of OPEC, to maintain a sense of solidarity against the industrial nations.

I am not myself upset when members of OPEC invest or buy shares in Krupp industries in Germany, or Kuwait seeks a portion of the Benz bonanza, or Saudi princes invest in real estate in London or California, or when Nigerian funds are carefully placed in western banks. All these are cases of counter-penetration.

If Nigeria had not effectively discovered that its oil could be a weapon to use in fostering enlightened western policies for southern Africa, and if Nigeria had not thus counterpenetrated western economies, the impact of Lagos on western policy-making would have been reduced accordingly.

I therefore do not agree with those Third World scholars and analysts who feel the Third World should actually dis-engage from the international capitalist system. It is too late to disengage. The northern industrialized countries hold the planet earth hostage. The industrialized countries could gradually destroy the world through pollution and other forms of ecological damage. Or the industrialized nations could impoverish the world by an indiscriminate and reckless depletion of resources. But the most ominous of all dangers is that the industrialized countries could destroy the world in a nuclear holocaust.

Given that the industrialized nations are now in a position to hold the whole planet earth hostage either to satisfy their industrialized luxuries, or in a catastrophic war among themselves, Third World countries simply cannot afford to pull out of the system. They must remain part of the system, but seek the kind of terms which would enable them to exercise greater influence over the northern hemisphere.

That is why it would be singularly irresponsible if we stopped the process which is now already increasing the influence of the Third World on the economic strategies of the northern hemisphere. The gains which OPEC has enabled the Third World to make must not be thrown away in a mood of militant abdication and withdrawal.

My sixth strategy is that of domestic austerity in the Third World. There ought to be greater circumspection with regard to consumption patterns, greater restraint in the importation of luxury goods.

There must also be a narrowing of the gap between the elites and the masses, a strategy of income distribution and, where appropriate, land reform.

But the austerity need not go to the extent of hampering the satisfaction of basic human needs. Efforts should be made to make possible minimum nutrition levels, minimum health care, minimum educational opportunities for children and the like. But ultimately the push in each developing country should be in the direction of discipline, restraint and austerity. It is often easier said than done, but experiments are already under way in places like Tanzania, Somalia, Mozambique and Guinea-Bissau.

The seventh strategy for transcending dependency is the transitional strategy of encouraging northern extravagance for the time being. In the immediate future it would be disastrous for the Third World if the United States and its allies succeeded in drastically cutting down the consumption of oil. An America self-sufficient in oil is an America invulnerable to external pressures. Indeed, the federal government in the United States has been urging Americans to be economical in oil partly for the reason that this would make the United States secure from external pressures.

And yet the United States itself exerts a variety of external pressures on other societies. True interdependence in the world requires mutual vulnerability to each other's pressures. If the northern industrialized countries can play havoc with the economies of Third World societies just by drinking less coffee than they did the previous year, or using less copper this decade than last, it is imperative that the southern hemisphere should also discover ways of exerting counter-pressures on the industrialized nations. Successful economies in petroleum consumption by the developed states must be prevented at all costs.

The British philosopher, Bertrand Russell, used to say that civilization was born out of the pursuit of luxury. What Russell might have added is that civilization declined sometimes out of the pursuit of excessive luxury. The current extravagance in the consumption of oil by the United States, and even the exceptionally high standard of living in western Europe as a whole, might have reached the stage of excessive luxury. The decline of western civilization might well be at hand. It is in the interest of humanity that such a decline should take place, allowing the different segments of the human race to enjoy a more equitable share not only of the resources of the planet but also of the capacity to control the march of human history.

I am not of course recommending the total collapse of western civilization. That too would be disastrous for the human race, for it is a civilization that has enhanced man's control over nature, enriched man's own creativity and inventiveness, and deepened man's understanding of the ultimate and the spiritual.

The West took the technology of production all the way from the spinning wheel to computerized manufacture. The West took the technology of destruction all the way from the bow and arrow to the neutron bomb. And the West took the technology of communication all the way from smoke signals to electronic and satellite media.

But these achievements had their costs and their distortions. The technology of production, symbolized by the civilian factory, became a declaration of war on nature. The northern industrialized countries engaged in reckless depletion of resources and damage to the environment, from pollution of rivers, lakes and the sea to threats to the ozone layer.

If the technology of production declared war on nature, the West's technology of destruction was inevitably a declaration of war on man. The arms race and the competition among northern industrialized countries attained new heights of sophisticated destructiveness. The search for new forms of annihilation continues to keep Soviet and western scientists constantly in a state of exhilarated competition for the ultimate secrets of a future holocaust.

The technology of communication, ranging from electronic media to publishing, has become at times a declaration of war on ultimate values. Human aggression and an enjoyment of violence have been sustained and nourished by the abuse of television and film.

Restraints on avarice and acquisitiveness have been undermined by the very ethos of capitalism as communicated and overcommunicated through its own instruments of dissemination.

The natural human weakness of lust has at times been recklessly exploited by the West's technology of communication, with negative consequences for the sacred drive of sexuality.

The West's technology of communication has at times undermined in Africa the imperative of moral reciprocity among people. Western culture has eroded some of the principles of collective responsibility in village life and tribal mores.

And finally, the West's technology of communication has often distorted the balance of information and cognition between different societies. This is what the information gap is all about; what Nigerians know about Zambians is often derived from western news agencies and media. My information about what is happening in India currently is disproportionately from the British Broadcasting Corporation and *The New York Times*. The Third World feels constantly under northern scrutiny, spied upon, observed, analysed, sometimes manipulated by the barrage of northern media. There is very little counterpenetration by Third World media into the centres of news and gossip within the northern hemisphere.

Given then that the western world and the Soviet bloc permitted the technology of production to become a declaration of war on nature and the environment, the technology of destruction to become a declaration of war on man, and the technology of communication to be a declaration of war on utlimate values, a partial decline of the civilizations of the northern hemisphere is a necessary precondition for creating a genuinely new international order. After all, the old territorial colonization was possible because the West controlled the means of destruction. As the English poet, Hilaire Belloc, put it:

> Whatever happens, we have got
> The Maxim gun, and they have not!

The newer forms of economic imperialism are perpetrated by those who control the means of production, sometimes acting through the medium of transnational corporations with their tentacles in different parts of the world.

As for cultural imperialism, this is best perpetrated by those who control the means of communication, from *Time* magazine to cowboy films, from the BBC to visiting professors at African universities.

As we indicated, Africa and the rest of the Third World cannot withdraw from the system without abdicating their responsibility for the planet as a whole. The Third World as a whole must therefore say to the northern hemisphere: "Let us renegotiate the terms of our coexistence on this shared planet. Let us sign a global treaty to help establish greater economic and social justice not only between men but also between societies." Thanks to the West's inventiveness, the clock of technology has indeed gone past the hour. It has ominous chimes of destruction. What is more it is an alarm clock, still ringing. "Ladies and gentlemen, it is time to wake up." In the new dawn the poor and the meek of Africa may not inherit the earth but, hopefully, they will finally inherit their own continent.

LECTURE 5

Patterns of Identity

In discussing the paradox of this particular lecture I am tempted to use an analogy from *Gulliver's Travels*, Jonathan Swift's satire. In size Africa is large enough to be worthy of a race of huge Brobdingnagians, but in fact the continent is inhabited by Lilliputians. We will remember that Brobdingnag was the country where the inhabitants were as tall as steeples, and everything else was in proportion. With 11½ million square miles, larger than any other inhabited continent apart from Asia, Africa is on the Brobdingnag scale. But Africans on the stage of world politics are specimens from Lilliput. Six inches high by world power standards.

One basic reason lies in Africa's fragmentation. The second largest inhabited continent of the world also happens to be the most fragmented.

Size has always been one of the measurements of power in the world system, the other measurements being resources, technology and military strength.

As we have indicated, Africa does have resources, but it lacks technology and a credible military capacity. As for size, the continent is large in square miles and is inhabited by more than 400 million people. But in world affairs the continent does not act as a unit; on the contrary it is subject to the weaknesses of its national, ethnic, ideological and religious cleavages.

Within the system of nation-states operating in the world today, size is less important than it once was in determining how safe a country is. But size is as important as ever in determining how influential a country is. A small country in the last quarter of the twentieth century need not be quite as fearful of its big neighbour as it might have been in the nineteenth century. It is true that the Vietnams of this world are still capable of invading a neighbouring Kampuchea, and the Chinas are capable of invading a Vietnam. But such events would have been happening more often in the nineteenth century in any case. What is distinctive about our present age of moral change is that smallness in size is less dangerous to a nation's survival than it once was.

On the other hand, because the world is now more intimately in communication with itself, and the globe has become a village in that sense, the larger members of the human community are in some ways even more influential than ever. It is partly because of this that the United States and the Soviet Union have become superpowers. It is also because of this that China may join them by the twenty-first century; and India will not be much further behind.

What has happened is that differences in size on the upper level of the scale have become more important than ever. Brazil's qualifications for future status as a major power include its size as the largest of the Latin American countries. It is second only to the United States in the western hemisphere in terms of size. On the other hand, no one is really expecting Great Britain ever to become a top-rank power again. It will be overshadowed in the course of the twenty-first century not only by countries like Brazil, India and China, but even by Nigeria if the country remains intact.

On the other hand, size at the bottom level of the scale matters less now than it did before for the reasons I gave earlier; the small powers are less vulnerable to arbitrary action by their big neighbours than they were a century ago.

African countries as a collection of Lilliputs are unlikely to be swallowed up again by external giants, though they themselves may fight with each other from time to time. But even their own internal wars are likely to be more accountable to a world looking in and to the censure of Pan-African judgement than similar conflicts might have been some decades earlier.

But Africa as a continent cannot be satisfied simply with being safe from direct colonization by others. That is truly the mentality of a Lilliput. African countries must begin to consider how effectively to influence others not merely on issues like the liberation of southern Africa but on issues that are truly global, such as the struggle for a fairer economic system in the world or the struggle for reduced nuclear danger to this planet.

A Lilliput is all right if all that it needs as a society is to recover its freedom and maintain it. But more general global policies are shaped by the superpowers of this world, the Brobdingnags of the world system.

But first let us examine why Africa is a continent of Lilliputs. Why is the region so fragmented? What is the nature of the fragmentation? What trends can we identify at the present time?

One could put together a symmetrical pattern of one to seven cleavages, and then take a leap to fifty and beyond. The symmetry in the form of an inverted pyramid begins with one continent, Africa; two permanent racio-cultural complexes, the Arab North and the black South; three religious systems, African traditional religions, Christianity and Islam; four dominant international languages, English, French, Arabic and Portuguese; five external hegemonic systems competing for either influence or profit within Africa, Western Europe, North America, the Sovet bloc, China and Japan; six political traditions partly fed by those five hegemonic systems and partly in opposition to those systems, liberal capitalism, socialism, nationalism, conservative traditionalism, militarism and Pan-Africanism; seven combat traditions, the warrior tradition, the jihad, passive resistance, guerrilla warfare, revolutionary terrorism, modern conventional warfare, and prospects for a nuclear option first in South Africa and later elsewhere in Africa.

As if this seven-tier structure of variation were not enough, we have in addition some 50 different countries in Africa and some 850 ethnic and linguistic groups.

And further there is the whole complex phenomenon of class formation and class struggle in Africa. New socio-economic groups are emerging from decade to decade, as new technology interacts with old cultures in the arena of resource utilization.

Of this multiplicity of crevices and cleavages, we are in this lecture particularly interested in five, namely: religion, ethnicity, ideology, nationality and class.

For the time being the weakest is the class cleavage. A Kikuyu peasant is probably Kikuyu first and a peasant second. In a confrontation between Kalenjin peasants on one side and the Kikuyu petty bourgeoisie on the other, the chances are that the Kikuyu peasant will side with his fellow Kikuyu regardless of class, rather than side with his fellow peasants regardless of ethnic affinity.

The distinguished Kenyan dissident, Jaramogi Oginga Odinga, wrote a book entitled *Not Yet Uhuru* (*Not Yet Freedom*). He belonged to the school of thought which saw the succeeding regime in Kenya as a case of continuing dependency. He tried to lead a movement based on class consciousness and dedicated towards basic land reform and social transformation. He expected the peasants and workers of Kenya to rally behind his Kenya Peoples Party. But when he turned around to look, his only followers were fellow Luo, of almost all classes. A movement which had been designed to be a truly proletarian creature suddenly discovered that it was naked and its ethnic organ was showing.

One question which arises is whether Jaramogi Oginga Odinga is contemplating writing a new book, *Not Yet Class Struggle*. He had once carried a message that was before its time. He thought he could mobilize class consciousness in defence of social and political transformation. He discovered people were still members of "tribes" first and members of social classes only secondarily.

And yet by the time this weary century comes to a close, class struggle will itself be part of the total scene of Africa's fragmentation. There will be a sharper perception of privilege and disparity and higher standards of social and economic justice. The modes of production will be more sophisticated, the lines of social cleavage more pronounced, the ends and purposes of society in greater dispute than ever.

When this century does indeed stagger out of time in sheer exhaustion, ethnicity in Africa should have declined, the state system might have got stronger and more consolidated, ideology more sophisticated and enriched, and religion on the defensive. But for the time being religion, ethnicity, ideology and the new state system have played a more decisive role than class in Africa's history.

Let us look at these other forces more closely.

Basically, Christianity is an Afro-western religion in the sense that almost all Christian nations are either in Africa or in the western world. Asia has millions of individual Christians, but apart from the Philippines there is hardly one Christian nation in the world's largest continent.

Islam, on the other hand, is an Afro-Asian religion in the sense that almost all Muslim nations are either in Africa or in Asia. There are indeed some Muslims in Eastern Europe, and Turkey is partly situated in Europe and partly in Africa. But on the whole the generalization holds, that Christianity is primarily an Afro-western religion and Islam an Afro-Asian religion. In terms of distribution the "Afro" is what they have in common, turning Africa into a potential ecumenical continent *par excellence*. Africa could become either the last theatre of a crusade between Christianity and Islam for the salvation of "black" souls or it could be the ultimate sanctuary of the ecumenical spirit, accommodating religious pluralism at its most tolerant.

Actually Africa's record on the religious front has so far been relatively impressive. We will remember that it was not until 1960 that the United States could divorce politics from religion sufficiently to elect its first Roman Catholic president, John. F. Kennedy. Yet in 1960 Senegal became independent with Léopold Senghor as the Roman Catholic president in an overwhelmingly Muslim country. The American electorate was not sure whether to trust a fellow Christian from another denomination, and remains unsure today whether this century it would ever elect a practising Jew for president. Yet the electorate of Senegal convincingly put its trust in Leopold Senghor in spite of the greater religious divide between Islam and Catholicism.

Tanzania, for that matter, has more Muslims than Christians. Yet Julius Nyerere has continued to enjoy decisive and convincing support from his compatriots across the religious divide. Julius Nyerere, like Léopold Senghor, is a Roman Catholic.

Many African families are multi-religious in composition without strain. One brother could be Muslim, another Roman Catholic, a sister Protestant and the father a practising member of a traditional African religion. Even in a country like Uganda, where religion has been politicized at times, from the 1890s until the present day, multi-religious families are quite wide-spread. The late king Mutesa II, who became Uganda's first president, often relied on the advice of his Muslim uncle, Prince Badru Kakungulu. Milton Obote, Uganda's second president, used to attend weddings and christening ceremonies of relatives from different religions. I once discussed with Idi Amin, Uganda's third president, his plan to let two of his children to be educated as Roman Catholics. Like many of Amin's plans, this one never came to fruition. But the fact that it was possible in Uganda for a Muslim president to proclaim the intention of educating two of his children as Roman Catholics was partly a reflection of Amin's own theatrical games, but was also in keeping with many precedents which had been set in Uganda over the years.

Uganda's fourth president was Yusuf Lule. He was born a Muslim, but embraced Christianity as an adult. He has remained an influential member of the Muslim side of his family.

Uganda's fifth president, Godfrey Binaisa, is a Muganda and a Protestant, like the first and fourth presidents. At least in terms of the wider extended family from which he springs, his background is also multi-religious.

I have illustrated solely from the presidential families of a country where religion has in any case been more politicized than in the majority of other African countries. And yet the ecumenical factor is striking and discernible.

The real reason for African ecumenicalism is simply the capacity of African traditional religions to tolerate and accommodate alternative religious cultures. Basically Africa had no religious wars before the Middle Eastern religions – Christianity and Islam – entered the continent. It is the rivalry between the Middle Eastern religions that creates potentialities for religious conflict in Africa. And yet those potentialities in turn are moderated by the underlying religious tolerance of traditional African creeds. These traditional African creeds did not have ambitions to convert the world. They were religions of particular ethnic groups, fundamentally important for those groups, but definitely not intended for export. Christianity and Islam, on the other hand, have been commodities for export from the first century of their existence. It is their competition in the marketplace of creeds which has generated the crusade syndrome over the centuries. In Africa this tendency has to some extent been mitigated or moderated by the more tolerant and less competitive character of the local religious heritage.

I am not saying that there has not been religious tension and even serious strife in Africa. What I am saying is that what appears to be religious strife is at times a reflection of other forms of strife. For example, in 1977 Archbishop Luwum of the Anglican Church of Uganda was apparently murdered on Amin's orders. Most of the world immediately concluded that he was murdered because he was an Anglican archbishop. But was it not equally possible that he was murdered because he was an Acholi? Idi Amin had periodically turned against the Acholi with ferocious genocidal sadism ever since he captured power in 1971. This was partly because the Acholi had been the largest single group in the army of Milton Obote, the man Amin overthrew, and partly because the Acholi had a reputation as strong warriors and dangerous adversaries. By the time the Archbishop was murdered he was one of the two or three most prominent Acholis still visible on the national scene in Uganda. Indeed, Archbishop Luwum was murdered alongside another remaining prominent Acholi, Mr Oryema, who was then a minister in Amin's government. The question persists, was the murder of the Archbishop sectarian or ethnic? It certainly was not as purely a case of religious victimization as the world press preferred to portray it.

The Sudanese civil war from 1955 to 1972 was also often described as a war between the Muslim north of the Sudan and the Christian south. In fact, only a small minority of southerners were in fact Christians. The great majority belonged to traditional African religions. In the ultimate analysis the Sudanese civil war was a war between the Arab and Arabized northern Sudanese, on the one side, and the non-Arabized black Sudanese to the south of them, on the other.

The Nigerian civil war from 1967 to 1970 was decidedly non-sectarian, in spite of Biafra's gallant attempt to portray it as a crusade between the Christian Ibo and Muslim northerners.

In the ultimate analysis, ethnicity is a more serious line of cleavage in black Africa than religion. Africans are far more likely to kill each other because they belong to different ethnic groups than because they belong to different religions.

Nor have the universalistic religions like Islam and Christianity succeeded so far in containing or transcending the tensions of parochial and ethnic rivalries. On the contrary, the universalistic religions have sometimes reinforced the parochial loyalties.

A particularly fascinating example concerns the relationship between Islam and the British colonial policy of indirect rule. Many Africana textbooks have simplified the distinction between French assimilation and British indirect rule. The picture is that the French tried to turn their colonial subjects as rapidly as possible into cultural replicas of the French themselves, whereas the British preferred to use the local native institutions and to permit considerable legitimacy for local cultures.

But although the difference between the two colonial powers was in reality not as sharp as the textbooks portray it, there was indeed a real distinction between the two.

Growing up in colonial Kenya under the British I was taught completely in my native language, Kiswahili, in my first three years at school. Had I been in a French colony I would probably have been plunged directly into the deep end of the French language from the beginning.

The British also facilitated the setting up of an interterritorial languages committee in East Africa to help in standardizing the pronunciation, orthography and development of African languages. Institutions of that kind and with those terms of reference were almost unknown in French Africa. The French were far less interested in preserving or developing indigenous African institutions and traditions than the British were.

But what has Islam got to do with all this? My own thesis is that the British policy of indirect rule was born out of a marriage between Islam and the Anglo-Irish philosopher, Edmund Burke. In a sense, the legacy of Edmund Burke is what British political culture is all about. As a rule of political prudence Burke advised: "Neither entirely nor at once depart from antiquity." If a society does aspire to change direction, it would be a mistake to do it either totally or in one sudden move. Political prudence, according to Burke, requires political sensitivity to history. As he put it again: "People will not look forward to posterity who never look backward to their ancestors."[1]

British political culture is a reflection in part of this broad political philosophy. The British are reluctant to turn their

---

[1] *Reflections on the Revolution in France* (1790), *Works* (London: World's Classic Edition, 1907), Vol. IV, p. 109.

back on antiquity either entirely or at once. So they maintain ancient institutions and modernize them as they go along, and they are slower to modify traditional habits than many of their peers.

This same Burkean gradualism in British domestic political culture came to influence British colonial policy. Indirect rule was based on a Burkean principle of gradualism. Many colonial policy-makers felt convinced that you could not persuade Africans to look forward to posterity unless you respected their tendency to look backward to their ancestors.

But British indirect rule assumed the presence of defined institutions in African societies, rooted in the history of those societies. And yet many African societies were relatively decentralized, without the state-like institutions of authority that the British would have preferred to use for purposes of governing.

Where was indirect rule to find its paradigmatic formulation? Lord Lugard, the architect of Britain's policy of indirect rule, found those institutions in the emirates of northern Nigeria. As Lord Hailey came to put it in his classic, *An African Survey*:

> It was in northern Nigeria that this procedure of using Native Authorities was given a systematic form by Lord Lugard during the years which followed the declaration of the Protectorate in 1900. The area which was brought under British protection was the scene of the most effectively organised system of indigenous rule to be found south of the Sahara. Most of the old-established Hausa Kingdoms had embraced the Islamic faith, and under its influence there had by the early 16th century developed a well-organised fiscal system, a definite code of land tenure, a regular scheme of local rule through appointed District Heads, and a trained judiciary administering the tenets of the Mohammedan law.[2]

The Fulani, who gained the ascendancy in the greater part of the Hausa country, used and helped to develop further this organized system of administration.

And then Lugard and the British came. In the words of another writer, Cyril Whitaker:

[2] Lord Hailey, *An African Survey*, (London: Oxford University Press, rev. edn., 1957), pp. 453-4.

Like the Fulani conquerors Lugard perceived that a solution for his problems presented itself in the form of the already effectively functioning system of government, which by then offered such obvious additional advantages as religious justification for authority, a formal code of law (the Islamic Shari'a), specialised judicial institutions, a more centrally controlled apparatus of administration, the custom of taxation, and, above all, the people's habit of obeying state authority. . . .[3]

In other words, the legacy of Islam in northern Nigeria, implanted several centuries before the British took over, provided a fertile ground for the implementation of the legacy of Edmund Burke in a colonial setting. The British were going to use the native institutions for imperial control, and were going to ensure in northern Nigeria that the people were neither entirely pushed nor at once pressured into turning their back on their own antiquity. A colonial doctrine was born within the wedlock of Burkean philosophy and Nigerian Islam.

While British indirect rule lasted it was in many ways humane and liberal, to the extent to which it did not seek too rapidly to impose an alien culture on an African people. It preferred to use figures of authority already trusted by the local population, rather than importing young and excessively enthusiastic district commissioners fresh from Oxford schools and Cambridge tripos.

But the question has often arisen whether Britain's relative toleration of African traditions (as contrasted with almost all other alien conquerors that Africa has had to deal with) was in the long run a disservice to Africa. Did it preserve ethnic differences between groups now condemned to live together by Britain within new territorial boundaries?

In Nigeria the other universal religion, Christianity, also played its part in sharpening ethnic differences. On the one hand, the missionaries were discouraged and often excluded from Muslim areas in the north by direct governmental policy and the British administration. On the other hand, the missionaries were allowed free play among those who were considered "pagans". One result was that the difference between the Hausa

<hr>

[3] C. S. Whitaker Jr, *The Politics of Tradition: Continuity and Change in Northern Nigeria, 1946-1966* (Princetown: Princetown University Press, 1970), pp. 26-7.

in the north and the Ibo in the east was in time no longer simply that one group was Hausa and the other was Ibo. There arose the additional distinction that the Hausa were mainly Muslim and the Ibo mainly Christian. And there was the third distinction that because the Ibo had been more exposed to missionary activity and had therefore gone to missionary schools, they had learned more of the western educational and verbal skills than the Hausa had done. In terms of those western skills, the Hausa gradually began to look as if they were "backward" or "pre-modern".

What all this in turn amounts to is a deepening of ethnic consciousness as a result of the impact of Islam among the Hausa and Christianity among the Ibo. Far from Islamic and Christian universalism diluting or transcending ethnic parochialism, those two global winds of Islam and Christianity helped to fan the flames of ethnic suspicions.

The stage was set first for the appalling slaughter of the Ibo in northern Nigeria in 1966, and later for the Nigerian civil war itself from 1967 to 1970.

As for secular ideological differences among Nigerians, these are still modest. Political parties are more likely to respond to ethnic and regional symbols than to ideological slogans as such. But again the question now arises whether ideology is assuming a new importance in African politics. Well, is it?

The most important ideological developments of the 1970s in Africa were the emergence of Marxist regimes in former Portuguese Africa and Ethiopia, on the one hand, and the partial revival of political liberalism in western Africa, on the other. Let us take each of these developments in turn.

Karl Marx himself expected socialist revolutions to take place in the more advanced of the capitalist countries. The irony of Marxism in Africa in the 1970s is that it was embraced by Ethiopia, a country just beginning to emerge from archaic feudalism, and also embraced by the former colonies of Portugal, which was itself the most backward of all the European powers that had ruled Africa. It looked as if the most fertile ground for Marxism in African conditions was either indigenous historical retardation as in the case of Ethiopia, or the impact of a backward imperial power like Portugal on its own colonies.

By contrast, Britain was at the time of colonialism the most advanced of the European powers controlling Africa. And yet for the time being not a single country previously ruled by Britain in Africa has gone Marxist. In the 1970s the most radical of the black African states previously ruled by Britain was thought to be Nyerere's Tanzania. Yet African Marxists would regard Nyerere's policies of *ujamaa* (socialism based on African concepts of familyhood) as either a sham or a case of false consciousness. Many of Tanzania's own radicals on the campus of the University of Dar es Salaam would at best regard Nyerere's work as a mildly progressive effort and Nyerere as at best a relatively progressive bourgeois.

Here then we have the two sides of the spectrum: former Portuguese colonies all emerging into independence highly radicalized on the one hand, and former British colonies remaining relatively bourgeois two decades after their attainment of political independence. The former Portuguese colonies had reacted precisely against a combination of Portugal's political retardation and the lengthy sway of Portuguese fascism. The British colonies, by contrast, had been dealing with a relatively sophisticated capitalist country, with a highly developed liberal democratic tradition. The former British colonies have not so far felt impelled to embrace Marxism on the rebound.

France as a colonial power was nearer to Britain than to Portugal in sophistication and capitalist advancement, but in colonial times it was definitely below Britain from that point of view. And so, whereas all former Portuguese colonies emerged radical, and no former British colonies did so, one or two former French colonies have become radicalized, though the great majority remain in a comfortable collaborative relationship with their former masters in Paris. The most consistently radical of the former French colonies has been Sékou Touré's Guinea. The country adopted the Leninist principle of "democratic centralism" and proceeded to construct what to many people has appeared to be a basically Stalinist regime.

In the 1980s it is conceivable that the ideological pattern in Africa may change. One or two former British colonies may indeed be tempted to go Marxist. Some people expect Zimbabwe to go Marxist if the Patriotic Front prevails. That is by no means certain, but in principle it is at least one scenario. What is clear so far is that the impact of Britain on her former colonies has not included the kind of reaction in the colonies which leads to the adoption of Marxism as the ideology of the newly independent states.

On the contrary, there are indications of some partial if fitful revival of liberal democratic thinking in former British West African countries. It will be remembered that Britain first bequeathed the Westminster model to her former colonies, and then witnessed its collapse in one African country after another. The liberal democratic model of more than one party in competition with each other, civil liberties in terms of freedom of expression and organization, and an independent judiciary, fell victim to two African trends in the 1960s: first, the attraction of centralized government and the one-party system and, secondly, the intervention of the military in politics. Certainly the one-party state was widely eulogized, and regarded as Africa's distinctive approach to democracy.

But since then disenchantment with military rule has led to renewed interest in the open society and pluralism in the context of a multi-party system. The people of Ghana and Nigeria definitely seem keen on returning to liberal democracy and civilian rule. The old songs of a one-party system are no longer as popular. It remains to be seen whether the soldiers of those countries will genuinely permit the process of redemocratization to take place.

Winds of liberal democratic change are also blowing through parts of former French Africa. I was privileged to interview President Léopold Senghor of Senegal for these Reith Lectures. He talked with pride about the restoration of inter-party competition in Senegal, with four parties recognized by the constitution. The trends recognized were Conservative, Liberal, Socialist and Communist. President Senghor discussed the new flexibility for newspapers, and the ease with which additional newspapers could be established provided they were not subsidized from abroad. He assured me of the independence of the Supreme Court in Senegal, estimating that in some periods the Supreme Court has rejected an average of six out of every ten decisions that have come before it from lower courts. Many of these findings of the Supreme Court are contrary to the wishes of the government.

While in Senegal for my Reith Lectures research I also interviewed a number of opposition leaders, including those whose parties are not recognized by the constitution. These leaders criticized the system strongly. There is no doubt that Senegal is not yet a truly open society. But it is significantly more open than most of its neighbours. The very fact that the opposition leaders spoke so bitterly and so strongly to a stranger, denouncing their president, was itself some indication that the system was not as repressive as the average regime in Africa.

Winds of liberal change have even been blowing through Sékou Touré's Guinea. Touré has not of course dismantled his structure of democratic centralism, nor has he done enough yet to attract back the one-fifth of his country's population whom he has driven into exile. But reports in the last year or so show evidence of liberalization within the system, accompanied by the release of large numbers of political prisoners.

But liberal democracy did not completely die in West Africa even in the worst days of civilian and military dictatorship elsewhere. In former British Africa little Gambia has maintained an uninterrupted tradition of political openness and and pluralism. In former French Africa there have even been experiments that combined competitive elections with a continuing military factor in politics. The case of Upper Volta is intriguing from that point of view.

To conclude this part then, it seems clear that the most distinctive trends ideologically in West Africa in the 1970s have included a liberal revival, while the most important ideological shift in southern Africa was the emergence of Mozambique and Angola as Marxist states. In the Horn of Africa both Ethiopia and the Somali Republic have maintained their relative radicalism, though their foreign policies and choice of external allies have fluctuated.

As for the rest of Africa, the ideological picture is mixed. Uganda is undergoing political changes since the fall of Idi Amin; Kenya is under a new president since the death of Kenyatta; and questions are being raised about the need for ideological and systematic change in Zaire.

Zambia's Kenneth Kaunda represents a genuine groping for a new ideology which transcends nationalism. Kaunda calls his ideology "humanism". It is difficult to be sure how socialism is supposed to relate to humanism in Kaunda's thought. Is socialism a stage towards humanism, something intermediate before full human empathy is achieved? Or is socialism an aspect of humanism? The two are not of course the same. After

all, Karl Marx regarded capitalism as a stage towards socialism;
but that did not make capitalism an aspect of socialism in
Marx's sense.

There is a third question. Is socialism in fact an alternative
to humanism as an ideology for Africa? The two might be both
progressive and acceptable, but constituting different options.
Under this last arrangement Kaunda could be a humanist
and Nyerere a socialist, and the two could be both progressive
and in alliance.

Again for these Reith Lectures I was privileged to spend
about two and a half hours with President Kenneth Kaunda
in Lusaka in July 1979. He spoke frankly about how some of
his peers used to pull his leg about his idea of "humanism".
Julius Nyerere jested with Kaunda, telling him that his "humanism" was popular with the West because it was ultimately soft on
western interests. Kaunda denied that humanism was a soft
vision in that sense. And I'm sure he would deny that his moves
to nationalize western mineral interests in Zambia were partly
caused by the taunts of his friends like Julius Nyerere. But
ultimately Kaunda is a pragmatist caught in the turmoil both
of the political upheaval of southern Africa and the economic
disarray of the copper market. Between this copper devil and
the deep blue sea of regional conflict Kaunda has had to make
adjustments to reconcile ideology to reality.

But in our conversation I was particularly intrigued by his
belief in world government. Not many heads of state in the
world subscribe to that vision, and very few heads of state in
Africa have the time to indulge in such ambitious futurology.
His belief in world government enabled me to begin to see why
he called himself a "humanist". In his view violence in man as
a species can ultimately be controlled only through a combination of two things, the self-restraint of the individual person
on one side and the global discipline of the world authority
on the other. He had once been a devout Ghandian, subscribing
to satyagraha as the force of discipline of the soul. He was converted to passive resistance as a strategy of struggle for freedom
and justice.

Sometime before Zambia attained independence Kaunda had
occasion to enter into a long discussion with an Indian who had
worked closely with Mahatma Gandhi. The two political figures
spent long hours discussing how a social order based on non-

violence could be established. Towards the end of their conversation the Indian said to Kenneth Kaunda: "Our states today are violent by nature. When you have won your independence are you going to take part in your country's government or are you in principle going to refrain from participating in it as Mahatma Gandhi did?"

Kenneth Kaunda replied as follows:

> To begin with, I do not think I can reach the state of perfection both in soul and body that Mahatma reached. Secondly, even if I could reach half his perfection I would not have the same personal influence on the government that will be formed in our Republic, once it is born, that Mahatma Gandhi had over the majority of Indian people and their leaders. I prefer therefore to work within the government in the hope that one may have better chances of changing things when one is part and parcel of the crew in any given statecraft.[4]

President Kaunda recited this anecdote to me, and later also gave me a copy of the two parts of his publication *Humanism in Zambia* in which the anecdote is also mentioned.

It is true that states are violent. When Kaunda became head of state he discovered before long the need to use violence. This included the utilization of violence to suppress the fanatical religious movement of Alice Lenshina in 1964. In desperation as the fanatics killed and maimed, President Kaunda virtually gave his security forces a *carte blanche* to use as much counter-violence in suppressing the movement as the security forces deemed necessary. This included instructions to shoot to kill. Kaunda was indeed caught up in the dialectic of a state trying to monopolize the legitimacy of the use of physical force within its boundaries. In pursuit of that monopoly the state is often driven to utilize violence against its own citizens.

Given then the fact that Kaunda is attracted to the theory of non-violence and its moral implications on the one hand, and on the other is forced to recognize that the state system of the world is fundamentally violent in its tendency, it is not surprising that the President of Zambia has veered towards a belief in world government. His two principles of individual self-restraint on the one hand and global authority on the

---

[4] For the anecdote see Kenneth D. Kaunda, *Humanism in Zambia and a Guide to its Implication* Part 2, p. ix.

other begin to appear as interdependent. He seems to some extent resigned to the persistence of at least certain forms of violence in Africa, and indeed in the world, for as long as the state system persists. And given that there are states in the world, someone has to head them. He is one such head, in spite of a deep-seated revulsion against violence.

This brings us to the cleavages of statehood and nationhood in Africa not just in relation to Kaunda's thinking, but as part of the sentence of fragmentation that for the time being Africa has to serve. As the "second decade" of Africa's independence comes to a close, important questions still remain about the political viability of the new territorial entities. Three forms of political violence are part of the story. Primary political violence concerns the very *definition* of the political community: with whom am I really prepared to share citizenship in all its facets? A civil war which results from an attempt by one ethnic or geographical unit to secede from a country whose boundaries were set by European colonial powers falls into this category. The Nigerian civil war and the Sudanese civil war both arose out of a profound dissatisfaction with the inherited frontiers of nation-hood, just as did the American civil war a century earlier.

Secondary political violence concerns the *purposes* of the political community: what goals should be pursued by the community and its members? This type of violence can also result in a civil war, especially if the different groups are ideo-logically divided, and if each seeks to control the centre at whatever cost. The Spanish civil war in the 1930s falls into the second category since it was concerned with the issue of who should control Madrid and rule Spain, rather than with the boundaries of Spain. On the other hand, the Basque separatist civil war in Spain while it lasted was a case of primary strife.

In Ethiopia the overthrow of the emperor was originally a case of secondary conflict, deciding who should control the country. But the war in the Ogaden and the continuing conflict in Eritrea are cases of the very definition of Ethiopia as an entity. Should it be divided up?

Tertiary political violence concerns the physical, social and wider political *environment* of a given community. Violence caused by demographic pressures, or a drought, or by a fall in international prices of primary commodities, is tertiary violence in this sense.

Ethnicity and the political geography of post-colonial Africa are part of the structure of conflict in the continent. Had northern Uganda which produced both Obote and Amin been part of the southern Sudan, the history of Uganda would certainly have been dramatically different. Had Rwanda and Burundi, which have experienced genocidal conflict between the Hutu and the Tutsi, been handed over to the British to be ruled as part of Tanganyika after the First World War, relations between the Hutu and the Tutsi would not have led to the scale of violence of the last twenty years. After all, they would not have been condemned to live with each other alone within the same territorial states of Rwanda and Burundi, but would have become part of a wider country which is today Tanzania. Indeed, the Tutsi and the Hutu, being culturally related, might even have been relatively united against other Tanzanians in the arena of competition for scarce resources. What is more, neither group would have had a military establishment with which to brutalize the other.

Unfortunately, our understanding of the interplay between ethnicity and political boundaries is still so imperfect that hindsight is still our greatest geography master.

But as the 1970s are coming to a close some old questions about Africa and its boundaries still persist. How dangerous are the artificial state frontiers created by imperial experience? How unstable is the ethnic mixture within each African country? What is the interplay between ethnicity and state boundaries?

One of the closing illustrations of border conflicts in the 1970s was the military confrontation which broke out between Uganda and Tanzania from October 1978 to April 1979. Before long there was indeed evidence that the president of Tanzania, Julius Nyerere, had launched a doctrine of *Pax Tanzaniana*. This was a doctrine of pursuing peace and stability in other countries under the auspices of Tanzania.

Pax Tanzaniana had points of comparison with *Pax Britannica*. The British had once aspired to consolidate peace and terminate tribal warfare through British initiative. Similarly, as I argued in an East African newspaper at the time of Tanzania's invasion of Amin's Uganda, Tanzania had indeed a record of struggling for peace and justice in other lands under Tanzanian leadership, even if it involved intervention or interference.

Sometimes there has been no disagreement among Africans. In southern Africa *Pax Tanzaniana* has been part of Tanzania's leadership of the front-line states. This has been widely accepted in Africa.

There was also a time when *Pax Tanzaniana* sought to influence the destiny of Nigeria. Mwalimu Nyerere recognised Biafra in April 1968. Mwalimu was seeking a solution to the Nigerian civil war. He was on the side of the separatists in that primary conflict.

In the Seychelles from 1977 *Pax Tanzaniana* apparently took the form of supporting the rebels against the founding fathers of independence. Tanzania was accused of having subsidized the coup that overthrew the government which inherited power from Britain at independence.

Even earlier, *Pax Tanzaniana* helped to realize Nyerere's manifest destiny. It contributed to the incorporation of Zanzibar into the body politic of Tanganyika. Intervention by Dar es Salaam helped to decide the fate of Zanzibar. A new hybrid state was born, the United Republic of Tanzania (Tanganyika and Zanzibar).

Then there was Tanzania's decision to close the border with Kenya, to teach Kenya a lesson, and, some would argue, to create sufficient instability in Kenya for a change of regime. In the case of Uganda, Tanzania sought to punish the Amin regime militarily. In the case of Kenya, Tanzania has attempted to teach the government in Nairobi a lesson through economic means. The Mwalimu of Tanzania — and let us remember that the Swahili word *mwalimu* does mean "teacher" — has often lived up to his name, dispensing lessons both to distant and neighbouring states.

The original purpose of Tanzania's invasion of Uganda was probably modest. Nyerere was going to do to Amin's Uganda what China did to Vietnam, that is, invade the country to demonstrate the superior power of the invader and then withdraw with the satisfaction of having administered a lesson. But Nyerere and Tanzania's forces soon discovered that they were not encountering much opposition from Amin's rabble army. It seemed to be a walkover. What started therefore as a mission very much like China's limited invasion of Vietnam become more like Vietnam's invasion of Kampuchea. In the case of the latter invasion the purpose was not simply to teach a lesson and then withdraw, but was actually to change the government in the capital city. Nyerere's forces, with their Ugandan supporters, were caught up in the momentum of easy victory over Amin's disintegrating war machine. The road seemed to be open all the way to Kampala with relatively minor opposition.

Tanzania's invasion of Uganda was unprecedented in the history of Africa since independence. The question it has raised is whether it constitutes a precedent of one African country invading another in order to change the regime in power. A qualitative modification may have taken place in the structure of the state system in Africa. Tanzania may only be the first of new sub-imperial powers in the continent. *Pax Tanzaniana* may have imitators in the years ahead. Fears of this kind were certainly expressed quite forcefully at the first meeting of the Organization of African Unity following the successful capture of Kampala by Tanzanian forces and their Ugandan allies. It remains to be seen whether the Organization of African Unity will introduce changes in its own machinery, and perhaps even establish a security apparatus of its own strong enough to reduce if not completely eliminate the danger of major military invasions between African countries themselves in the years ahead.

What confronts Africa is a choice between a system of collective security and a system of international vigilantism. An African High Command or a police force under the Organization of African Unity would be a structure of Pan-African security. A number of French-speaking African countries have recommended such a structure, especially since the 1977 invasion of the Shaba province of Zaïre by opponents of President Mobutu operating from Angola. Moroccan troops formed the nucleus of the African force which replaced the French troops in war-ravaged Shaba after the invasion.

The King of Morocco and the President of Senegal, among others, felt that it was time for Africa to establish its own machinery of continental law enforcement.

Among those who opposed the Moroccan and Senegalese initiative was the President of Tanzania, Mwalimu Julius Nyerere. Nyerere had his own good reasons for opposing a Pan-African security system of the kind recommended by the francophone states. These reasons included Nyerere's suspicion of France as an invisible prompter behind the francophone stage.

Nevertheless, the idea of a Pan-African security system could have been examined independently of the controversy surrounding the role of France in suppressing the anti-Mobutu invaders of Shaba province. By opposing the proposed Pan-African force, Julius Nyerere helped to reduce the options available to the Organization of African Unity in matters of collective security.

The only viable alternative available was international vigilantism of the kind Tanzania embarked upon when it invaded Uganda and toppled the regime of Idi Amin in 1979.

But what is vigilantism? Americans should know, and according to two American analysts:

> [vigilantism] consists of acts or threats of coercion in violation of the formal boundaries of an established socio-political order but intended by the violators to defend that order from some force of subversion. . . . When individuals or groups identifying with the established order defend it by resorting to means in violation of these formal boundaries, they can be usefully denominated as vigilantes.[5]

Under this definition Julius K. Nyerere is an international vigilante. He violated international law partly in order to return Uganda to the rules of international decency. He helped to terminate arbitrary rule in Uganda by resorting himself to an act of international arbitrariness. The American frontier in the old days of the American West had "vigilante committees", as they were called, consisting of a group of citizens committed to the maintenance of law and order by summary proceedings.

Julius Nyerere does not believe in summary justice in his domestic policies. He is in reality a liberal democrat with a socialist veneer. But Nyerere has practised summary justice in his foreign policy. The economic actions against Kenya and the military invasion of Amin's Uganda are his most striking exercises in international vigilantism.

But can one blame Nyerere? Is not the whole area of Africa's international relations still a case of an untamed frontier? Is there not a need for vigilantes?

[5] H. Jon Rosenbaum and Peter Sedenberg (editors), *Vigilantism* (Philadelphia: University Press, 1976).

I myself would not worry very much if every African vigilante was Julius K. Nyerere, humane, sophisticated, and sensitive to the wider implications of every act of policy. Nyerere
may commit major international blunders from time to time
(including his recognition of Biafra in April 1968) but his
heart is probably in the right place.

Unfortunately, we cannot guarantee that every international
vigilante that Africa produces will be a Julius K. Nyerere. It
would be a greater service to Africa if Nyerere joined those
francophone African voices which are groping for a continental
system of collective security. Nyerere's involvement would
itself reduce the danger of this Pan-African security involvement being manipulated by France behind the scenes.

A marriage is required between Kwame Nkrumah's old idea
of an African High Command designed to keep imperialist
invaders at bay and the newly proposed Pan-African force
designed to put the African house in order. Africa needs to
be protected both from external enemies and from internal
deviants.

There is a crying need in the continent for collective military
self-reliance. The rise of Cuban influence in the 1970s in Africa
was definitely one symptom of this need. Here was a continent
of over 400 million people, seemingly dependent militarily on
an island of less than 15 million people thousands of miles
away. On issues like Zimbabwe many Africans have regarded
as their ultimate weapon the importation of Cuban troops to
tilt the balance. This is a humiliating confession of Africa's
military impotence. Here was a continent with large armies
scattered in different societies, but armies better at repressing
their own societies than at liberating the rest of the continent.
Why were Cuban troops necessary to stem the South African
challenge in Angola in 1975 and 1976? There were, after all,
enough African states in sympathy with the Popular Movement
for the Liberation of Angola. Why did they not put their
armaments where their mouths were, and get ready to intervene
on behalf of the MPLA?

The Organization of African Unity has recognized the special
role of the front-line states in southern Africa in terms of diplomatic initiatives. Before long, the OAU should also support the
front-line states in terms of military defence. Some of these
states have already suffered militarily from the white-dominated

regimes. Reprisal raids into the front-line states will get worse in the future when the wars of liberation engulf the Republic of South Africa itself.

Protecting Africa from external enemies and internal deviants needs more than vigilante exercises from time to time. It needs the political will to transcend Africa's own fragmentation and establish a capacity for self-defence, for self-pacification and ultimately for genuine self-development.

Perhaps late in the twenty-first century an eyewitness from our own present-day Africa of Lilliputs will be giving evidence to a newly vindicated and sophisticated African Brobdingnag. Our present-day pettiness and quarrels may well amaze the mighty Africa of tomorrow.

I do hope that the mighty king of tomorrow's Africa is not so flabbergasted by the accounts he receives from the eyewitness of the twentieth century that he explodes in words which echo Jonathan Swift's judgment on his own century. Lemuel Gulliver, describing England and Europe to the King of Brobdingnag, provoked His Majesty into making the following famous observation about Europeans of his day: "By what I have gathered from your own relation . . . I cannot but conclude the bulk of your natives to be the most pernicious race of odious vermin that nature ever suffered to crawl upon the surface of the earth."

If Gulliver's compatriots crawled into Africa and infected me and my compatriots, Africa must find ways of transcending the conflict-ridden heritage of Europe. In terms of size and cohesion let Brobdingnag be our temporary model, our measurement of stature in the twenty-first century and beyond.

LECTURE 6

In Search of *Pax Africana*

I first developed the concept of *Pax Africana* when I was working on my doctoral thesis[1] for Oxford University in the early 1960s. I was concerned with Africa's capacity for self-pacification. The question which was often put at that time in the wake of decolonization was: "Now that the imperial order is coming to an end, who is to keep the peace in Africa?"

In my view, self-government implied above all self-policing. The logical conclusion of the whole process of decolonization lay in Africa's ambition to be its own policeman.

In this lecture I would like to carry my concept of *Pax Africana* one stage further. It is not enough that Africa should have a capacity to police itself. It is also vital that Africa should contribute effectively towards policing the rest of the world. It is not enough that Africa should find the will to be peaceful with itself; it is also vital that Africa should play a part in pacifying the world.

In my first lecture I discussed the crisis of habitability in Africa. The Garden of Eden is in decay, and inadequately suitable for political habitation. But are we sure the world as a whole is habitable enough for the human species? On issues like the balance between resources and population, are we gambling with the future? Are we depleting the resources of

[1] My doctoral thesis was later published under the title of *Towards a Pax Africana: A study of Ideology and Ambition* (London: Weidenfeld & Nicholson and Chicago: University of Chicago Press, 1967).

this planet too precipitously? In our stockpiles of nuclear weapons, are we constructing our own Gehenna? In short, are we living too dangerously?

If one part of the world is not habitable enough politically, the flow of refugees gets under way. But if planet earth is not habitable enough, we cannot stop it to get off. We cannot become a new race of boat people, floating in outer space, running away from a global Vietnam.

It is for these reasons that the world needs a policeman. The four crises endangering the planet are depletion of our resources, expansion of the population of the world, pollution and other dangers to the ecology, and large-scale violence among human beings.

From Africa's point of view, the first danger of the depletion of resources is tied up with problems of dependency and under-development. Africa is not in adequate control of its own resources. Indeed, the net beneficiaries of Africa's resources lie outside the African continent. Many of its mineral resources help to industrialize the rest of the world without necessarily improving the African condition itself. We have explored some of these issues in earlier lectures.

With regard to the risk of the population explosion, it cannot entirely be divorced from economic justice in the world. My closest friend in Mombasa fathered more than a dozen children before his wife died a few years ago. Half of those children have themselves also died. With such a high level of infant mortality, I never even attempted to persuade my friend that he and his wife should have aimed for a smaller family. His answer would have been: "How would you know which children would survive?"

My friend is a poor man, proud and self-reliant. Partly because of that his children were in part his insurance. I have never had the bad manners to question his judgement about a large family, close and intimate as we have been for twenty years. I have seen him grieve for some of those children as they have died. All I have been able to do is to name one of my own sons after him, in desolate admiration of a father in adversity.

In like manner, I do not think the western world should go around preaching small families to poverty-stricken Indian peasants. The western world need not name their children after these peasants, but the West should stop planning for even higher standards of living for its own children. The moral duty of every family in the northern hemisphere is not to leave its children materially even better off than they have been, but to plan for a slight impoverishment of the next generation of westerners. The western world already consumes far too much of what there is on the planet, without planning for much more.

I personally would not mind seeing some continuing extravagance in the western world, but this is only a transitional strategy designed to weaken it sufficiently to make it responsive to the demands of global reform. Until those reforms are agreed to by the West and the Soviet Union and its European allies, I do not want to hear western preachers beaming their sermons on population control to my friend in Mombasa. I would rather westerners and Soviet citizens took a vow of abstinence, committing themselves to the deliberate reduction of the standards of living of their children after them.

As for the dangers to the environment, the greatest threat comes from the industrialized countries. The Japanese are great eaters of fish but they are also great wasters of fish. I have walked along the shores of Japanese waters and have been appalled by the dead fish washed ashore by the waves, victims of water pollution. I have witnessed comparable sins in California and in some of the lake areas of Michigan. In the north of England where I received part of my education I have indeed witnessed the ugly face of industrialism, amidst humane and warm human beings.

All these three dangers to our planet — depletion of resources, expansion of population and damage to the ecology — need institutions of global supervision and control. But the worst danger of them all is large-scale human violence, including the danger of a nuclear war. This is the fourth crisis of global survival, and will command special attention in this lecture.

Why am I addressing myself to this one instead of the three others? Well, partly because war is human destructiveness in a purer form than depletion of resources, expansion of population, and even damage to the environment. People deplete resources usually for production or consumption, rather than directly in order to destroy. Countries expand in population because many of its citizens want children and even love them.

Damage to the environment is usually a regrettable side-effect of more legitimate processes. But the systematic compiling of weapons of mass destruction is not incidentally negative. It is directly and purposefully negative — designed to destroy at its worst millions of people upon pressing the button of an intercontinental ballistic missile.

This is where *Pax Africana* looms into relevance. Is Africa affected by this nuclear cloud hanging over the world's political system? How does Africa suffer from it, and in what way can Africa contribute towards saving the world from a nuclear holocaust?

This brings us to the paradox of Africa's location. Africa is the most centrally located of all continents, but politically it is perhaps the most marginal. This anomaly has implications for *Pax Africana*, as we hope to demonstrate.

Let us first grapple with the political geography of Africa. Physically on the globe, regardless of whether one uses the Mercator projection or another one, the African continent is firmly central. As we indicated earlier, it is the only continent that is cut almost in two halves by the Equator. It is also the only continent which is traversed by the Tropics of both Cancer and Capricorn. It is bounded by the two busiest oceans in maritime and trade activity, the Atlantic Ocean and the Indian Ocean. To its north lies the biggest and busiest land-bound waterway in the world, the Mediterranean Sea.

Africa's centrality has other dimensions as well. Among the oldest is once again the commercial factor. This goes right back to Vasco da Gama and the effort to find a sea route to India. Circumventing the African continent by way of the Cape was part of this process of facilitating Europe's maritime communication with Asia.

The route around Africa remained important for Euro-Asian communications from the days of the spice trade to the industrial revolution. Later on, the Cape would serve the cause of rubber from Malaya, jute from India, wool from Australia, meat from New Zealand, and, in the opposite direction, textiles and industrial equipment from Europe to those countries.

By the 1970s the Indian Ocean carried virtually a quarter of Britain's trade, and an even higher percentage of Japan's. The bulk of the exported oil also needed the two basic African routes, either through the Suez Canal or around the Cape of Good Hope.

The strategic importance of the Indian Ocean also increased the significance of Africa. The Soviet Union is a bi-continental state, which needs the Indian Ocean partly to communicate with itself. The United States has had nuclear submarines in the Indian Ocean covering Soviet cities. Britain's loss of such traditional military bases as Suez, Aden, Singapore and Gibraltar, have also increased the functional alternative provided by a western presence in the Indian Ocean. Once again this has helped to consolidate Africa's strategic relevance.

This is quite apart from the many critical minerals and other resources located within Africa itself, which we discussed in a previous lecture. The location of the continent is certainly pregnant with implications for much of the trade and traffic of the world, and therefore for much of the industry of the twentieth century.

And yet, in spite of this centrality of location physically, Africa is marginal in influence and power within the global system. What are the causes of this marginality? And can the marginality be transcended?

Some of the causes of Africa's relative political weakness in the global scheme of things have already been touched upon in the previous lectures I have given in this series. Africa's crisis of habitability and political stability creates uncertainty and somewhat fluid conditions. Political institutions are fragile and often collapse under the weight of local rivalries. This situation does not enhance Africa's leverage in the world system.

The legacy of Africa's humiliation across the centuries is still with us, conditioning the attitudes of outsiders towards Africans, and often also conditioning the level of Africa's political resolve. Outsiders do not take Africa's influence as yet seriously, and Africans themselves have not acquired enough self-confidence in global diplomacy.

The crisis of acculturation, creating an African leadership still imitative of the West, groping for new ideologies and a new sense of direction, basically dependent in outlook — this cult of acculturation has also undermined Africa's capacity to innovate.

Then there are all those crevices and cracks of Africa's fragmentation, leaving the continent divided by a multiplicity of territorial boundaries, a wealth of ethnic and linguistic divisions, a diversity of competing ideological and political traditions and a triumvirate of religious traditions. This basic fragmentation of the continent is part of its general weakness in world affairs. But there is one advantage in a fragmentation of Africa which produces some fifty different members of the United Nations and its agencies. The multiplicity of votes has increased Africa's leverage within the United Nations system. It is true that voting power is only a modest form of power in a world dominated by military and economic might, but nevertheless African ambassadors are sought after in any resolution before such institutions as the United Nations General Assembly, the General Conference of UNESCO, the meetings of the United Nations Conference on Trade and Development and other world organizations.

Then, as we indicated, there is Africa's burden of underdevelopment: immense mineral resources in the continent, great agricultural potential, alongside some of the lowest standards of living in the world. This is a condition which cannot but detract from Africa's impact on contemporary world history.

But in the ultimate analysis, Africa's marginality in the global arena can be reduced to three major weaknesses: technological underdevelopment, organizational incompetence and military weakness.

As we indicated, the resources are there in abundance within the continent, and their rewards could be distributed more evenly between different parts of the continent. But where resources are abundant but development is modest, one reason is technological inadequacy. As compared with many Asian countries, African countries manufacture very little themselves and are in command of only the most rudimentary technological capability. Transnational corporations have been among the major carriers of western technology into Africa, but the level has still been rather modest as compared with the comparative technological sophistication that is encountered in countries like Korea, Taiwan and even Pakistan in Asia, on one side, and countries like Mexico, Chile, Argentina and of course Brazil on the other side of the Third World.

Then there is Africa's organizational incompetence. Such inefficiency is by no means unique to Africa. It is certainly widespread in much of the Third World, and has examples on a reduced scale in the First World of advanced capitalist countries and the Second World of advanced socialist countries. Nevertheless, the level of incompetence in Africa organizationally is sometimes staggering. This is aggravated by political instability, social corruption and the whole crisis of moral ambivalence arising out of the bubbling of the cultural melting pot.

What is corrupt and what is not is sometimes a function of competing moral systems within the same society. When I was Dean of Social Sciences at Makerere University in Uganda, I sometimes used to receive letters from one relative or another making a special plea that his son be admitted to Makerere in spite of the fact that he had not done so well in the School Certificate examination. Then, to make the case clearer, my correspondent would proceed to remind me of his relationship with me in terms of the extended family. What was to be understood, without necessarily being spelled out, was that in matters of university admission, as in everything else, charity did indeed begin at home.

Any relative who wrote to me in those terms was not necessarily trying to corrupt me. The relative was operating within one moral system of mutual support and fellowship. But the university institution in Uganda was a product of another culture altogether, western culture, and carried with it a different moral system which presumed the sanctity of merit as a basis of university admission. I, as an African Dean in an African university, was caught up between two moral worlds. I then had to explain to my relatives the constraints within which I was operating, and hoped that they would understand that I could not give priority to candidates on the basis of ethnic nearness or family relationship.

But I am sure that on other occasions I might have made a concession or two to the older morality. Certainly many Africans have had to grapple with that moral ambivalence, and large numbers have capitulated to ethnic nepotism. This has been part of the crisis of relative incompetence and disorganization in the context of modern conditions.

After technological underdevelopment and organizational weakness, there is also Africa's military marginality. In a way, this was what imperialism was all about. V. I. Lenin argued that imperialism was the "monopoly stage of capitalism". It is at least as arguable that imperialism was the monopoly stage of *warfare*. Implicit in concepts like *Pax Britannica* was the assumption that western powers had special privileges for being armed to the teeth, while at the same time proceeding to disarm the natives. It was readily assumed that western powers were civilized enough to initiate world wars, but Africans had to be stopped from waging tribal conflicts. In the words of Jomo Kenyatta, written way back in the 1930s:

> The European prides himself on having done a great service to the Africans by stopping the "tribal warfares" and says that the Africans ought to thank the strong power that has liberated them from their "constant fear" of being attacked by the neighbouring warlike tribes. But consider the difference between the method and motive employed in the so-called savage tribal warfares and those employed in the modern warfare waged by the "tribes of Europe" and in which the Africans who have no part in the quarrels are forced to defend so-called democracy.[2]

It is to be remembered that Kenyatta's complaint was *before* the Second World War. Therefore it was of course also before the nuclear era in the military field. The question which now arises is whether the Non-Proliferation Treaty, designed to minimize the number of countries that have a nuclear capacity, and ultimately intended especially to discourage Third World countries from going nuclear, could conceivably be regarded as an extension of the old philosophy of "imperialism as a mono-poly stage of warfare". Those who have already acquired the necessary capacity now assume the role of preachers telling others not to acquire that capacity while they themselves retain it.

Pressures by the United States especially on countries like Pakistan, Brazil and India, trying to prevent them from acquir-ing a nuclear capacity, are a typical example of the assertion that nuclear sauce is only for northern geese, and not for southern ganders.

The Non-Proliferation Treaty assumed extra urgency in the late 1950s and early 1960s as more and more countries in Asia and Africa became independent. I was in Uganda when the

[2] Kenyatta, *Facing Mount Kenya* (First published, London: Secker & Warburg, 1938; Heinemann Educational Books, 1979), p. 212.

government of Dr Milton Obote decided to sign the Non-Proliferation Treaty. Although the chances of Uganda's acquisition of a nuclear capacity were at the time remote, and continue to be remote, I believe Dr Obote made a mistake. He should have remembered all those treaties of renunciation that African rulers had to sign during the European scramble for Africa, treaties between African chiefs and European powers, designed for "pacification" and European control.

President Obote should indeed have remembered the Ugandan Agreement of 1900 signed between the King of Buganda and the British Government. The British started the gradual process of demilitarizing the local rulers. The British imposed a gun tax, just as there was a hut tax. The gun tax was applied to any person who possessed or made use of "a gun, rifle, pistol, or any weapon discharging a projectile by the aid of gunpowder, dynamite, or compressed air".

On the other hand, "the possession of any canon or machine-gun is hereby forbidden to any native of Uganda including the kings of the country".

As regards exemption from the gun tax, the following was the provision of the Agreement between the Kabaka (King) of Buganda and the Government of Great Britain.

> The Kabaka will be credited with 50 gun licences free by which he may arm as many as 50 of his household. The Queen Mother will, in like manner, be granted 10 free licences annually by which she may arm as many as 10 persons of her household. . . . Chiefs of counties will be similarly granted 10 annual free gun licences; all other members of the Lukiiko or Native Council, not Chiefs of counties, three annual gun licences, and all landed proprietors in the country, with estates exceeding 500 acres in extent, one free annual gun licence.[3]

The pacification of Buganda by the British was now under systematic and quantifiable control.

By 1962 Uganda had become independent. The old rules concerning guns and how many were to be owned tax-free by which official now depended upon the new government

---

[3] For the text of the Uganda Agreement of 1900 see Appendix II in D. Anthony Low and R. Cranford Pratt, *Buganda and British Overrule* (London and Nairobi: Oxford University Press, on behalf of the East African Institute of Social Research, 1960), pp. 350-66.

of sovereign Uganda. And yet here was some new device called the Non-Proliferation Treaty, asking the new chiefs of Africa to engage once again in a form of military renunciation which the big powers themselves were not eager to embrace for themselves.

The new African chiefs capitulated with even less reason than the previous chiefs of the beginning of the century and of the previous century. The new presidents of Africa did not have to sign that treaty on threat of some kind of reprisals as their ancestors signed away their rights to Queen Victoria. The Non-Proliferation Treaty is supposed to be a voluntary act of self-denial.

From a Third World point of view, I do not believe the treaty is worth the paper it is written on. And if I were to become president of a Third World country, I would not hesitate to withdraw from it. Imperialism in the nuclear age is the monopoly stage of nuclear technology. Those who insist on monopolizing nuclear know-how for themselves are heirs to *Pax Britannica*, seeking to end tribal wars in distant lands while arming to initiate world wars from their own heartland.

From Africa's point of view this whole business concerning nuclear proliferation is linked to a fundamental interplay between the warrior tradition, technological change and the whole doctrine of non-alignment in world politics.

The warrior tradition in Africa's experience declined partly because it came into confrontation with a superior military technology. In 1941, against a background of what came to be the Second World War, a distinguished friend of Africa reminded Africans of Europe's might and its role in Europe's expansion. In a book addressed to Africans, Margery Perham said:

> Let it, therefore, be admitted upon both sides that the British Empire, like others, was obtained mainly by force. Even where there was no serious fighting, news of victories nearby, or the fear of stronger weapons was often enough to persuade tribes to accept the rule of the white strangers . . . African tribes, backward, disunited, weak, were helpless before Europe, especially since the perfection of the machine gun.[4]

[4] Margery Perham, *Africans and British Rule* (London: Oxford University Press, 1941) pp. 53-4, 60.

This history of Africa's military weakness has continued to haunt African leaders and thinkers. As President Sékou Touré once put it: "It was because of the inferiority of Africa's means of self-defence that it was subjected to foreign domination"[5]

This triumph of western military technology created important changes in the cultural field as well. Among the casualties over time were the aims and rituals of the warrior tradition in many African societies. The warrior tradition was associated with two interrelated processes, the attainment of manhood and the attainment of adulthood. Manhood involved all the symbolism of the sexual division of labour, complete with the hard masculine virtues of physical courage, physical endurance and even purposeful ruthlessness.

Adulthood, on the other hand, was endowed with a different set of virtues and values, pre-eminent among which was social responsibility combined with adult self-reliance.

But under the western impact the warrior tradition in Africa was badly damaged by two terrors which had come with the white man, the terror of gunfire and the terror of hellfire. The terror of gunfire was what the new military technology of the white man was all about. Those early primary resisters in Africa who attempted to stop European occupation discovered before long the overwhelming superiority of the cannon as against the spear, the gun as against the bow and arrow. European technology soon overrode and demoralized the resisters. The new terror of gunfire initiated the decline of the warrior tradition.

That decline was made worse by the terror of hellfire which came with Christianity. Death for millions of Africans was now given a new meaning. African ancestors were cut down to size, denounced as insignificant by the missionaries of the new religious order.

In addition, Christianity had damaged the warrior tradition by proclaiming the ethic of "turning the other cheek". Meekness was regarded as a virtue even for otherwise virile and valiant men. As we indicated in a previous lecture, a version of Christianity which had hardly ever been truly implemented in Europe, and which had in part become anachronistic on

---

[5] Conakry Home Broadcasting Service, 7 June 1965. See BBC Monitoring Service Records of Broadcasts in Non-Arab Africa.

its home ground, was now bequeathed to African school children and peasants. The God of Love was mobilized behind the mask of "imperial pacification". The message of Christianity discouraged Africans not only from fighting each other but also from resisting the colonial presence.

While the warrior tradition when it was alive had enabled individual Africans to attain adulthood, the new dependency converted whole societies into children. The warrior tradition had been a process of individual maturation; the new dependency was a collective retreat into childhood. The imperial powers decided to regard themselves as guardians and trustees; the colonies were condemned to the status of wards. X-films in Mombasa began to display the sign: "Not to be shown to Africans and children under 16."

What all this meant was not simply the abolition of the warrior tradition as an effective initiation into manhood and adulthood for the individual. Imperialism both emasculated societies by suppressing the hard virtues of physical courage and endurance, and forced them to retreat from maturity and adulthood.

And then independence came. A brief sense of having rematured intermingled with the celebrations. A euphoria of having rediscovered collective adulthood permeated the atmosphere on the day the flag was raised.

But what about the warrior tradition and the right to bear arms? A partial resurrection took place as soldiers captured power in one African country after another. A high proportion of African nations fell under the control of people who were, to all intents and purposes, tribal warriors wearing modern uniforms.

But the relationships between the northern industrial countries and the southern countries of Africa and elsewhere in the Third World retained a paternalistic component. The issue of whether armaments should be permitted to flow freely within the Third World continued to be a point of debate within industrialized countries. Should the arms trade be controlled? Should the Soviet Union and the United States reach an agreement on limiting arms supplies with the Third World? The whole debate smacked of the paternalism of *Pax Britannica*.

For a while, Africa itself was ambivalent about rearmament. This was partly because of earlier conceptions of the whole doctrine of non-alignment. As one African country after another became independent, a duty envisaged for each of them was that of helping to moderate the tense relations among the great powers. The first conference of independent African states held in Accra, Ghana, in April 1958, appealed to the great powers to discontinue the production of nuclear and thermonuclear weapons and to suspend all such tests "not only in the interests of world peace but as a symbol of their avowed devotion to the rights of man". The meeting reaffirmed the view that the reduction of conventional armament was "essential in the interests of international peace and security", though the conference went on to condemn "the policy of using the sale of arms as a means of exerting pressure on governments and interfering in the internal affairs of other countries".[6]

Non-alignment in those early days was still seduced by the ideals of disarmament. This was partly because of India's ambivalence on the precise relationship between non-violence and non-alignment. The two most important Indian contributions to African political thought were the doctrines of non-violence and non-alignment. Gandhi contributed passive resistance to one school of African thought; Nehru contributed non-alignment to almost all African countries. As Uganda's Milton Obote put it in his tribute to Nehru when he died, "Nehru will be remembered as the founder of non-alignment. . . . The new nations of the world owe him a debt of gratitude in this respect."[7]

But how related were the two doctrines of non-alignment and non-violence? For India itself Gandhi's non-violence was a method of seeking freedom, while Nehru's non-alignment came to be a method of seeking peace. And yet non-alignment was in some ways a translation in foreign policy of some of the moral assumptions which underlied passive resistance in the domestic struggle for India's independence. Gandhi himself once said: "Free India can have no enemy. . . . For India to enter into the race for armament is to court suicide. . . . The world is looking for something new and unique from India . . . . With the loss of India to non-violence the last hope of the world will be gone. . . ."[8]

[6] Consult the declaration of the First Conference of Independent African States (15-22 April 1958), Appendix: C. Legum, *Pan-Africanism* (London: Pall Mall Press, 1962 edition), Appendix 4, pp. 147-8.

[7] *Uganda Argus*, Kampala, 29 May 1964.

[8] *Harijan*, 14 October 1939.

In spite of Gandhi's vision, independent India did not practise abstinence. Gandhian non-violence was not fully translated into a foreign policy. Suspicion of Pakistan in particular was too strong to permit that.

And yet of all the countries in the world, India under Nehru came nearest to symbolizing the search for peace. For a crucial decade in the history of Africa and Asia, India was the diplomatic leader of both continents. And in the doctrine of non-alignment she bequeathed to many of the new states a provisional foreign policy for the first few experimental years of their sovereign statehood.

With that policy the wheel of global pacification had come full circle. Asia and Africa had once been colonized partly with the view to imposing peace upon them. But now non-alignment had turned the tables on old concepts like *Pax Britannica*. It was now those who were once colonized who were preaching peace to their former imperial tutors.

And yet India's non-alignment was destined to go nuclear. India was indeed the first non-aligned country to explode a nuclear device. This happened in 1974.

India was also the first country without a permanent seat in the Security Council of the United Nations to explode a nuclear device. The first five nuclear powers were precisely the war lords with the veto in the Security Council: the United States, the Soviet Union, Great Britain, France and China. India at last broke this neat equation, and put the issue of nuclear proliferation onto a new footing.

But is nuclear non-alignment a contradiction in itself? Should Africa and the other Third World countries continue in their older tradition of distrust towards militarism? If one of the ambitions of non-alignment continues to be the effort to moderate tensions in the world, then two Third World legacies have to go nuclear. One is the legacy of Nehru in India and the other is the legacy of the warrior tradition in Africa. The nuclearization of non-alignment would mean not merely using nuclear power for peaceful purposes, but using that power to reduce the danger of East–West convulsion.

The nuclearization of the warrior tradition, on the other hand, would imply a reassertion of adulthood in the Third World, a rejection of the imperial monopoly of warfare. Non-alignment would seek to reduce tensions; the warrior tradition would seek to reduce dependency.

We know that India has already moved into the nuclear field. For the time being, India has assured the world that it will use its nuclear capacity for peaceful purposes, though at the same time it has warned that such a non-limitary commitment would partly depend upon Pakistan's nuclear policy in the years ahead. But how far is Africa from a comparable nuclear role and in what way would proliferation of nuclear weapons beyond India into Africa be a contribution to global pacification?

Militarily, Africa is still a dependent continent in terms of weaponry. Apart from the white-dominated countries in the south, and to some extent apart from Egypt, the technology of making weapons is for the time being a distant aspiration for African countries except on an extremely modest scale.

Next to dependence in weaponry, there is dependence in capital for the purchasing of weapons. Liberation movements in Africa have more often than not had to raise money outside Africa to buy arms from, say, the Soviet bloc. African states do make contributions to liberation, but in relation to the needs of the struggle these contributions are modest.

Thirdly, there is dependence in military training and advice. Again, a disproportionate share of the training that African armed forces need is dependent on external advisers and organizers. Many African officers are still sent abroad for this kind of training, while instructors from abroad are imported to prepare other officers and other ranks in Africa.

Fourthly, there has been dependence in military personnel from outside powers. Since August 1978 the estimate of the number of Cuban troops in Africa has ranged from 35,000 to 37,000. The French have maintained about 10,000 troops in different roles, though recent moves concerning the fate of Western Sahara and the civil strife in Chad have led to reductions in the French military presence. The Soviet Union has had nearly 7,000 military personnel of different kinds in the African continent.

In terms of using foreign troops in actual combat, the largest numbers used have been Cuban troops and French troops in different conflict situations.

But how is Africa to get out of this general political and military marginality which has persisted in spite of the continent's strategic location?

Technologically, the process will be slow, as Africa increases its absorption of technological know-how, learns also from its own indigenous techniques, and strengthens its training institutions and structures of research.

The struggle against organizational incompetence is fundamentally sociological, and may need a long period of social reform and cultural adjustment. Again, institutions of training and social research could make some kind of contribution, however modest, in the struggle against inefficiency, corruption and lack of adequate focus in planning and policy implementation.

But in the diplomatic arena the situation could be substantially eased when three African countries succeed in solving some of their internal weaknesses, and assume the continental leadership that they deserve. The triumvirate of African diplomatic power before the end of the century will consist of Nigeria, Zaïre and black-ruled South Africa.

Nigeria is of course a giant partly because of its population and, at least for the time being, partly because of its oil resources. With a population of approximately 80 million people, Nigeria is by far the largest country on the continent and likely to be the largest in Eurafrica as a whole before long, surpassing the German Federal Republic in population.

Zaïre is also a large country, larger in size than Nigeria, but the second or third largest in population south of the Sahara. In minerals it is particularly well endowed. Zaïre has more than 30 per cent of the non-Communist world's reserves of cobalt, over 70 per cent of its industrial diamonds, as well as 6 per cent of its copper, with some potential in oil and natural gas. If the country can put its house in order before the end of the century, transcending its chronic instability and infinite inefficiency, it could exercise considerable political leverage in the politics of the African continent. For the time being its potential influence is revealed mainly in its cultural impact, as Zaïrean music sets Africans dancing from Lusaka to Lagos.

The third giant of Africa will be black-ruled South Africa before the end of the century. The industrial base of the country is already immense, and its mineral wealth is striking. The country has 74 per cent of the non-Communist world's reserves of chromium, 49 per cent of its gold, 37 per cent of its manganese, more than 10 per cent of its uranium and 73 per cent of its platinum. There are variations in estimates of reserves, but I have preferred to use these estimates of the business world.[9] When this immensely rich, and relatively developed, economy passes into the hands of the majority of the people of that country between now and the end of the century, South Africa will of course take its place among the triumvirate of diplomatic leadership in Africa alongside Zaïre and Nigeria.

By that time South Africa will probably be a nuclear power, pushed to that status by the defensiveness of the white oligarchy while it lasted. But, as we indicated earlier, nuclear weapons are unlikely to be decisive in the fate of apartheid, since the main threat to the racial system will be from an internal revolution which is not susceptible to nuclear resistance. As we indicated, South Africa is unlikely to use nuclear tactical devices in the streets of Soweto, or even in the Bantustans, without substantially accelerating the exodus of the very whites that the nuclear strategy wants to save. After liberation and the introduction of genuine majority rule, South Africa's nuclear status will be more clearly an asset, unless the world has already denuclearized by then.

World peace in the coming decades may indeed depend upon the outcome of two processes: nuclear proliferation in the Third World and women's liberation in the northern hemisphere. This unlikely and disparate alignment of forces may well decide the destiny and even survival of the human race. Of course women's liberation is not uniquely western or northern. There are feminist movements in the Third World too, as some of the street demonstrations in Iran after the fall of the Shah demonstrated. But especially important for the peace movement is the northern women's struggle for greater participation in decision-making. After all, the most devastating war machinery lies in the north. The androgynization of the control of that machinery could help to change both its rules and its orientation.

On the other hand, the overwhelming majority of northerners (male and female, radical, liberal and conservative) is against nuclear proliferation in the Third World. The very instability of Third World countries creates alarm about the prospect of nuclearizing their military capabilities. This northern fear of Third World proliferation could be an asset to the peace

[9] See *Fortune* magazine's special map of Africa's resources, 14 August 1978.

movement. Some degree of nuclear proliferation in the Third World could be a necessary first step towards getting the North to agree to total and *universal* denuclearization in the military field.

But in order to understand more fully this *de facto* alignment between nuclear proliferation in the Third World and women's liberation in the northern hemisphere, let us examine seven traditions of combat in contemporary cultures.

The war mystique in contemporary cultures takes many forms, not all of them concerned with large-scale conflict.

Seven traditions of combat are particularly pertinent. In the Muslim world there may be a resurrrection of the jihad tradition, a commitment to defend Islam with the sword if need be.

Passive resistance, on the other hand, could be described as being in part a Christo-Gandhian tradition. This combines a commitment to social transformation with a renunciation of violence. Passive resistance often tends to include the cruci-fixion syndrome, the pursuit of martyrdom as a strategy of protest. The Christo-Gandhian tradition is, in some respects, culturally feminine.

Curiously enough, the Iranian revolution in its strategy against the Shah was Christo-Ghandian in inspiration, rather than derived from the jihad. Thousands of unarmed people poured out into the streets of Teheran in what was the most impressive people's revolution of the second half of the twentieth century. It was also the most impressive case of passive resistance since Mahatma Gandhi inspired the masses of India to rebel against the British Raj.

To that extent Ayatollah Khomeini was strikingly similar to Gandhi in his historic role. Both leaders mobilized cultural and religious symbols to move the hearts of their compatriots against what they regarded as unjust systems.

The Iranian revolution has moved from a Christo-Gandhian strategy to a more jihadic outlook since it captured power. The strategy of harsh justice is part of the origins of Islam. And the Iranian revolution has now opted for a nostalgic return to sacred ancestry.

The third tradition of combat in the modern world (after the jihad and passive resistance) is the wider one of the warrior tradition. It survives in a variety of forms in different cultures, from the Samurai code in Japan to the residual *Deer Hunter* image in the United States. The warrior tradition is based on the hard virtues of individual masculinity: toughness, courage, endurance and even purposeful ruthlessness.

The warrior tradition also survives in a variety of forms in Africa, sometimes disguised behind the uniform of a modern army.

The fourth combat culture operating in Africa and elsewhere, especially in the Third World, is the guerrilla tradition. It has been particularly important in struggles for national liberation and for social revolutions. Increasingly, this mode of combat is becoming *androgynous*, rallying both men and women to the struggle. The wars in southern Africa belong to this category.

A closely related tradition is just that of terrorism. This includes skyjacking, hostage-holding, blowing up bars and the like. But unlike a guerrilla movement, terrorism need not include a literal organized army, though it often does require "operators" and "agents".

Normal usage of the term "terrorism" is conditioned by the values of the power structure with a vested interest in "law and order" rather than in fundamental social reform. The word therefore tends to have negative connotations. But my use here attempts to be normatively neutral. Terrorism is a form of warfare rather than a form of deviancy. Just as there can be a just war and an unjust one, so there can be just and unjust terrorist movements.

Like guerrilla movements, revolutionary terrorism these days tries to be androgynous, recruiting both men and women.

On the whole, other forms of warfare destroy in order to incapacitate the enemy. Terrorism destroys in order to frighten the population. To incapacitate the war machine of the enemy is often more difficult than to erode the self-confidence of the population.

Terrorism is often the ultimate weapon of the weak, a strategy of last resort. Lord Acton was perhaps right in his statement, "Power corrupts; absolute power corrupts absolutely." But since his day we have indeed come to recognize in the twentieth century that powerlessness also corrupts, and absolute powerlessness leads on to acts of desperation. Terrorism is often born out of the agonies of frustration. That is what the bombs in the markets of Jerusalem and the pubs of Ulster are all about.

What should be remembered is that the power structure of a state can also become terroristic. The record of the British forces in Northern Ireland has had its moments of moral degeneracy, as the European Commission on Human Rights has at times been compelled to note.

But far more guilty of counterterrorism is the state of Israel, which has insisted on killing dozens of Arabs (no matter how innocent) for every Jew that has fallen in a terrorist act.

Marxist debates have long agonized over the concept of "state capitalism". It is time liberal debaters also recognized "state terrorism" as an aberration with a logic of its own even in liberal societies. The state of Israel is a classic case of a domestic liberal democracy that has produced a terrorist foreign policy. The periodic bombing of Lebanese villages by the Israelis has been a feature of this policy. The terrorist is not always the sly, disguised individual about to plant a bomb in a marketplace. The terrorist could be the ruthless state official who plans comparable acts against others, and gives orders that the acts be carried out under governmental auspices.

But "state terrorism" can sometimes be an aspect of the sixth tradition of combat. This is what is sometimes called conventional war, a confrontation between two organized armies, representing different societies, or different states, or different regions of the same society or state. This combat tradition also tends to be masculine *de facto*, though not always because of any conscious cultural logic.

If the guerrilla is symbolized by the Sten gun, the terrorist by the time-bomb, the more collective effort of conventional warfare is symbolized by the modern tank.

As for the seventh and most devastating tradition of combat, this is genocide. It is now globalized. It is what nuclear war is all about. The defence of New York requires the destruction of at least 40 million Russians in the ultimate analysis. The defence of Moscow requires the devastation of half of the United States.

The northern hemisphere has created a new form of genocide. It is partly masochistic since its primary targets are northerners themselves (Europeans, Americans and Russians).

But the new genocide is also a throwback to primeval murder, cool and premeditated. Only this is *homocide* rather than homicide. The destruction of the human race is at stake, rather than the destruction of "merely" a single human person.

The struggle against the new homocide is not "merely" about saving lives. It is more fundamentally concerned with saving life itself on this planet.

The Third World can force the north to retreat from the brink of this global genocide only by engaging in a nuclear Russian roulette for a short while. The Third World must briefly encourage nuclear proliferation as a strategy of shocking all nations (including the superpowers) to give up the nuclear game altogether. Big power opposition to nuclear proliferation is not merely a special case of military monopoly and imperialism. It also encourages the massive nuclear powers to underestimate the dangers of the game. Only when unstable Third World rulers acquire these dangerous toys will the superpowers be converted to total military denuclearization. Nuclear proliferation, dangerous as it is, is the inescapable culture shock needed to force a really fundamental reappraisal. Modern genocide thus demands a nuclear Russian roulette by the Third World to create a climate of hopefully manageable crisis. Only then will this most dangerous of the traditions of combat (the genocide tradition) be forced back from the brink of homocide.

The above seven traditions are on the whole products of a male-dominated world. The jihad and the warrior traditions are particularly inclined towards machismo, but the others are also basically led by men or dominated by them.

Passive resistance is sometimes inspired by the softer virtues often associated with femininism, patience, gentleness and even love. But when we call even this tradition "Christo-Gandhian" we reveal the genders of these founding fathers.

Revolutionary resistance (especially modern guerrilla and terrorist movements) aspires to be androgynous, but it has not quite made it yet.

Tyrants have sometimes been poisoned by their mistresses, but the setting is again often sexist. Women become instruments of male rivals competing for power. Conventional war pits spy against spy, tank against tank under male leadership.

As for the genocidal lunacy of the twentieth century (the 'sui-genocide' of potential nuclear war) the perpetrators have been overwhelmingly the males of this masochistic species.

What then is the way out?

The two greatest hopes for peace in the twenty-first century may lie in that strange alliance between nuclear proliferation and women's liberation.

As we indicated, the first trend, nuclear proliferation, is necessary in order to shock the superpowers into a state of emergency about denuclearization. For as long as the Soviet Union and the United States feel that they will maintain the control of the nuclear threat, so long will they maintain the complacency of SALT I and II. Strategic Arms Limitation Agreements are not intended to stop the escalation of the arms race. They simply seek to slow it down.

In fact what is needed is a speedy deceleration, a rapid reduction of our destructive capacity rather than a mere containment of further growth.

From this point of view, African countries should stop thinking in terms of making Africa a nuclear-free zone. This was a position which made sense at one time. President Kwame Nkrumah organized a "ban the bomb" international conference in Accra at the beginning of the 1960s, and considered an international march towards the Sahara in protest against French nuclear tests in Algeria before independence. Nkrumah regarded Africa at the time as a continent under the threat of two swords of Democles: racism and apartheid in southern Africa and the nuclear threat symbolized by the French Sahara tests in northern Africa. Nkrumah froze French assets in Ghana as part of the strategy against the nuclear desecration of African soil.

Nigeria broke off diplomatic relations with France over the Sahara tests. All this made sense at the time it was happening in the early 1960s. But for the 1980s and 1990s Nigeria should move towards making itself a nuclear power, unless steps are taken before then by the world as a whole to put an end to nuclear weapons universally.

It is true that on one side nuclear energy might seem to be dysfunctional to Nigeria since it is a rival to its own major mineral resource, oil. But the development of a nuclear capacity by Africa's largest country is probably a necessary precondition if Africa's diplomatic marginality is to be ended. Nigeria should follow the example of its fellow giants, Brazil in Latin America and China and India in Asia, and pursue the goal of a modest nuclear capability. My own reasons for suggesting such a capability have nothing to do with making Nigeria militarily stronger. The ultimate purpose is to make the world as a whole militarily safer. Only when the West and the Soviet bloc discover that they cannot make the rest of the world refrain from the nuclear dream unless they themselves give up the weapons, will the world at last address itself to the fundamentals of human survival.

Our third member of the triumvirate, Zaïre, may be further away from the organizational and technological capacity for nuclear status than either South Africa or Nigeria. But even Zaïre could not be ruled out of the game of nuclear power for very long. It was among the very first African countries to discover uranium, though its future nuclear programme may well necessitate the importation of uranium from other African countries.

To summarize the argument so far, Africa should give up the idea of promoting itself as a nuclear-free zone except in terms of keeping outside powers and external bases at bay. Those African countries that signed the Nuclear Non-Proliferation Treaty should reconsider their position, and estimate the chances of at least a continental consortium within Africa of nuclear energy, linked to a strategy of developing a small nuclear section in the military establishment of Nigeria for the time being, and in Zaïre and black-ruled South Africa later.

But the threat to humanity is not merely in nuclear weapons. It is also in war itself at the present stage of technological advancement. How do we change our values and perceptions fundamentally enough to drastically reduce the danger of war?

For the Marxist the answer lies in a world of transformed class relations. But is it not just as likely that the answer lies in a world of transformed sex roles? It may not have been entirely by accident that in cultures which have otherwise been vastly different from each other, war has on the whole been a disproportionately masculine affair. "Our warriors are our sons" — this has been the common theme of most combat cultures in history, both in Africa and elsewhere.

The question therefore arises whether a future mixture of sex roles, a new androgynous chemistry, might not result in a fundamental demilitarization of human culture at large. Will the greater participation of women in combat and in planning for war be itself a contribution towards reducing the danger of war? If warfare has been so strikingly male-dominated until now, and both the barracks and the prisons of the world reveal a disproportionate male presence among those who perpetrate violence, will a new combination of men and women in military establishments reduce the aggressive element in those establishments?

It is this consideration which has led me to believe that progress in women's liberation in the northern hemisphere may be as important for world peace in the future as the trend towards nuclear proliferation in the Third World.

Nuclear proliferation is a process of military democratization. It seeks to break monopolies in weaponry in the hands of the northern warlords. Nuclear proliferation also seeks to break secret societies based on forbidden nuclear knowledge under the control of the West and the Soviet bloc. But ultimately the best moral case for military democratization in terms of increasing participation in military nuclear technology in the world is whether this democratization will in turn ultimately lead to the drastic reduction of large-scale warfare in human affairs.

Women's liberation in Africa itself is taking place on a modest scale, but it is women's liberation in those lands guilty of perpetrating the largest magnitude of warfare in so far, that is the northern industrialized states, that may be particularly critical for human survival. It is because of this that I continue to affirm that world peace hinges in the ultimate analysis on the military ambitions of the Third World and the political aspirations of newly liberated women in industrialized countries. It is a strange alliance, an unconscious alliance in a historical process.

This alliance is at the global level. But within the Third World there is another level of joint action and concerted purposes. In the long run the alliance between the legacy of non-alignment and the tradition of the warrior might also contribute to the right equilibrium in world affairs. Gandhi's approach, very much like the approach of Jesus, emphasized the softer feminine virtues of love and patience, the mobilization of humility and compassion for social transformation. The warrior traditional has continued to emphasize the harder virtues of the masculine code, the ideals of courage and endurance, the romance of toughness in adversity. A fusion of these three traditions — non-alignment, Gandhi's legacy and warriorhood — could help create conditions for a more habitable planet earth.

For Nigeria, Zaïre and black-ruled South Africa, going nuclear would be a new initiation, an important *rite de passage*, a recovery of adulthood. No longer will the great powers be permitted to say that such and such a weapon is "not for Africans and children under 16".

As for the gap between the militarily powerful and the militarily weak, this will ultimately have to be narrowed, first by making the militarily weak more powerful and then by persuading the militarily powerful to weaken themselves. The road to military equality is first through nuclear proliferation in Third World countries, and later in global denuclearization for everybody. African countries will not rise fast enough militarily to catch up with even the middle-range northern countries, but African countries could rise sufficiently fast to create conditions for substantial disarmament in the world as a whole.

Africa is still on the periphery of the game of proliferation. In the move from the periphery to the main stream of action in the nuclear field, Africa will have to get out of its technological shyness and nuclear inhibitions.

When little white children misbehave in some western societies, the mother may sometimes say "Behave yourself — or a big black man will come and take you away." Today we are dealing not with little white children about to be threatened with the danger of a big black man, but we are dealing with white adults who must be threatened with the danger of big black men wielding nuclear devices.

Sometimes the threat of a black danger addressed to a little white girl did have the desired effect: the child would behave herself. The question which arises is whether the same threat addressed to the white grown-ups of Washington, Moscow, London and Paris — the ominous threat of nuclearized black power — will in time create enough consternation among the dangerous naughty white war planners of the northern hemisphere to induce nuclear sanity at long last.

The struggle itself may have two major historical areas of importance. For Africa the gap between physical centrality and political and military marginality will be narrowed. Africa under its triumvirate of diplomatic leaders, partly endowed with nuclear credentials, will have begun to enter the mainstream of global affairs. And the world as a whole, once it discovers the lunacy of its nuclear ways, will have learned an old lesson in a new context: the lesson that wild mushrooms are dangerous.

INDEX

DATE DUE

MR 1 8'82			
MR 1'83			
GAYLORD			PRINTED IN U.S.A.